Sharia as Informal Law

This book takes a comprehensive approach to investigate how Sharia influences and manifests in the everyday lives of young Muslims, aiming to unravel the meaning and relevance of Sharia-driven laws and practices in English-speaking Western societies. By focusing on the grassroots level, it provides a deeper understanding of the lived experiences of Muslims and their relationship with Sharia. The presence of Muslims in Western countries has a long history, with recent waves of migration and conversions contributing to their increasing numbers. This study recognizes the diverse nature of the Muslim community, comprising both migrants and local converts, who have become integral parts of the pluralistic fabric of multicultural societies. The research draws on in-depth interviews with 122 young Muslim individuals from diverse backgrounds representing three different Western countries: Australia, the United States, and the United Kingdom. Diversity of participants allows for a broader exploration of the Muslim community and the inherent diversity of opinions, interpretations, and practices regarding Sharia. This approach moves beyond theoretical debates, providing concrete insights into the practical implications of Sharia for young Muslims in their respective Western contexts. The book also sheds light on the evolving landscape of information and knowledge acquisition in the age of digital technologies and cyberspace. It explores how young Muslims access and seek knowledge in the twenty-first century, recognizing the impact of changing sources and modes of information on their religious practices and beliefs. This aspect adds a valuable dimension to the study, capturing the dynamic nature of knowledge dissemination and acquisition among young Muslims in Western societies. The book will be fascinating reading for academics, researchers, and policy-makers working in the areas of Law, Political Science, Minority Studies, Religious Studies, and Islamic Studies.

Ihsan Yilmaz is Research Professor and Chair of Islamic Studies at the Alfred Deakin Institute for Citizenship and Globalisation (ADI), Deakin University, Melbourne, Australia.

Sharia as Informal Law

Lived Experiences of Young Muslims in Western Societies

Ihsan Yilmaz

Routledge
Taylor & Francis Group
LONDON AND NEW YORK

First published 2025
by Routledge
4 Park Square, Milton Park, Abingdon, Oxon OX14 4RN

and by Routledge
605 Third Avenue, New York, NY 10158

Routledge is an imprint of the Taylor & Francis Group, an informa business

British Library Cataloguing-in-Publication Data
A catalogue record for this book is available from the British Library

ISBN: 978-1-032-76440-5 (hbk)
ISBN: 978-1-032-77351-3 (pbk)
ISBN: 978-1-003-48260-4 (ebk)

DOI: 10.4324/9781003482604

Typeset in ITC Galliard Pro
by Apex CoVantage, LLC

Contents

1 Sharia's Significance for Western Muslims

1.1 Introduction

This book undertakes an extensive exploration of the dimensions of Sharia in the lives of young Muslims residing in Western societies. Its primary objective is to deeply investigate the everyday relevance, significance, and practical application of Sharia-based informal laws and practices in the lives of young Muslims manoeuvring through the intricacies of Western cultures and legal systems. Through this endeavour, the book strives to cultivate a profound grassroots understanding of the essence of Sharia and its pragmatic implications for Muslims in English-speaking Western nations.

To achieve this ambitious objective, the book employs a research methodology centred on in-depth interviews with individuals from diverse backgrounds within the Muslim community. Engaging participants from three English-speaking Western countries – Australia, the United States, and the United Kingdom – the book illustrates the remarkable diversity within the Muslim diaspora and the varied ways in which Sharia manifests in their lives. These interviews serve as a means to illuminate the lived experiences of Muslims, presenting an authentic depiction of the diverse viewpoints, interpretations, and applications of Sharia within Western contexts.

The focus on young Muslims residing in Western societies adds more depth to this investigation. By exploring the lived realities of this specific demographic, the book sheds light on the evolving nature of Sharia and its adaptation to the modern challenges encountered by Muslims in the West. This exploration reveals the intricate dynamics between tradition and modernity, religious identity, cultural assimilation, cyberspace, and the nuanced negotiations undertaken by young Muslims in their pursuit of harmonious integration within Western societies.

Moreover, this book serves as an insightful departure from the commonly relied-upon sources of information about Sharia. Rather than depending solely on mainstream media portrayals, which often perpetuate misconceptions and stereotypes, or seeking explanations solely from religious scholars, this research provides an original and insightful perspective. By delving into the applied aspect of Sharia, as experienced and understood by young

DOI: 10.4324/9781003482604-1

Muslims themselves, this study endeavours to bridge the gap between academic discourse and real-life experiences. It offers a valuable opportunity to authentically understand the lived realities of Muslims in the West and their multifaceted relationship with Sharia.

Presenting a comprehensive analysis rooted in empirical research, this book aims to contribute to existing scholarship on Islam, informal law, and multiculturalism. It enriches academic discourse by providing a nuanced exploration of the practical implications of Sharia within the diverse and evolving landscape of Western societies. Furthermore, it underscores the importance of recognizing the diverse opinions, interpretations, and applications of Sharia within the Muslim community, challenging monolithic assumptions, and encouraging dialogue and understanding.

The presence of Muslims in Western countries holds a long history, with recent waves of migration and conversions contributing to their growing population. Whether through migration or conversion, these individuals have become an integral part of the diverse fabric of societies in countries such as Australia, the United States, and the United Kingdom. Acknowledging this multicultural reality, this study aims to explore not only the understanding and practice of Sharia or Islamic law among young Muslims but also the broader implications of these beliefs.

Rather than simply probing participants about their views on Sharia, this study explores various themes to understand how Sharia and Islamic law influence young Muslims' perspectives on democracy, community leadership, and civic participation. It examines how these individuals navigate the pursuit of religious knowledge and confirmation, exploring the diverse avenues they utilize to acquire and validate information within their faith.

In essence, this book transcends a mere exploration of young Muslims' acceptance or rejection of Sharia. It endeavours to spotlight how their decision-making processes are influenced by Islamic teachings. It explores how young Muslims navigate their religious freedom within the legal and constitutional frameworks of their respective countries, often through the practice of informal laws. This concept of "informal law" does not necessarily run parallel to formal legal systems but rather acts as a complementary force, shaping aspects of their lives.

For instance, voting, considered a constitutional right and obligation by many, illustrates how Islam encourages political participation and voting, showcasing how legal pluralism can complement the lives of young Muslims. This approach to understanding Sharia as an informal law that may or may not shape the lives of the participants adds a distinct perspective to the study.

Additionally, alongside examining the significance of Sharia in the lives of young Muslims, this book investigates the evolving landscape of knowledge acquisition and information-seeking. It explores how the sources and methods of accessing religious knowledge have evolved for young Muslims in the twenty-first century. This exploration of the dynamic nature of knowledge-seeking among young Muslims contributes a novel dimension to the book's overall analysis.

1.2 Muslim Informal Law in the West

Laws in the socio-legal sphere manifest in various forms and shapes. While formal state-driven laws hold an official and authoritative position, they are not the sole legal framework followed by citizens and communities. Informal laws, although lacking institutionalization and legitimation by the state, continue to be relevant, particularly within diverse communities (Yilmaz 2016, 2022). This highlights the limitation of a state-centred approach, which tends to be uniform and monolithic, often overlooking the needs and complexities of citizens and groups with intersectional or plural identities.

Within the broader spectrum of legal systems, it is worth noting that laws extend beyond the parameters defined by the state. Religiously motivated or inspired laws serve as a prominent example of this phenomenon. They operate alongside formal laws and are informed by faith traditions and religious principles. Additionally, other factors such as ethnicity, regional location, and cultural norms shape informal laws. These informal legal mechanisms, derived from cultural, religious, and communal contexts, often provide alternative avenues for addressing legal issues and meeting the specific needs of certain communities.

In fact, one could argue that formal laws themselves have evolved through a process influenced by cultural and ethical near-consensus. Over time, societies have re-evaluated certain practices, recognizing their shortcomings and inherent injustices. This has led to the transformation and adaptation of laws to align with changing societal values and norms. For instance, the widespread ban on capital punishment in many countries today can be attributed to a cultural and ethical understanding that deems it problematic, while in the past, it was considered a normal practice.

Within pluralistic societies, ethnic minority groups often rely on informal laws as formal legal systems may not adequately address their unique cultural, religious, and communal needs. The existence and recognition of these informal laws contribute to the concept of legal pluralism. It is important to emphasize that legal pluralism does not imply a direct conflict between informal and formal laws supported by the state. Instead, it recognizes the coexistence and interaction of multiple legal mechanisms within a society to accommodate the diverse requirements and practices of different communities.

Legal pluralism can be understood as the existence of different legal mechanisms concurrently operating within a particular society. Vanderlinden (1971) defines it as "the existence within a particular society of different legal mechanisms applying to identical situations" (p. 19). Griffiths (1986: 1) describes it as a state of affairs in which behaviour guided by more than one legal order occurs within a specific social field. This perspective underscores the dynamic and multifaceted nature of legal systems, reflecting the diverse norms, values, and traditions within a given society.

To illustrate legal pluralism in action, one can examine South Asian countries like India and Pakistan, where the legal system recognizes the acceptance of informal laws for religious minority communities, particularly in matters related to family law (Yilmaz 2016, 2019). These communities often adhere to their own religiously grounded legal frameworks alongside the formal state legal system. This recognition of religiously inspired informal laws acknowledges the significance of cultural and religious diversity within these societies and aims to provide legal accommodations and protections that reflect the unique needs and aspirations of minority communities.

In both Western contexts and Muslim-majority countries where Sharia is not formally integrated into the legal system, the practice of Sharia-driven principles represents a form of legal pluralism (Yilmaz 2002). However, there is no singular, universally defined Sharia law or its definitive source. Sharia is a complex and multifaceted concept that encompasses a broad range of interpretations and applications. Various sources, such as hadith (sayings and actions of the Prophet Muhammad), the Quran, the practice of the Prophet and his companions, and diverse traditions, contribute to the shaping of Sharia (Yilmaz 2020).

Sharia holds deep significance for many Muslims as it provides a comprehensive framework for guiding their personal, social, and legal lives. Hoffman (1993) notes that Sharia law represents an all-encompassing order that governs every sphere of life, including aspects as seemingly mundane as etiquette and social norms. It serves as a moral and ethical compass, providing guidelines for personal conduct, family matters, business transactions, and more. For many Muslims, adherence to Sharia is not only a matter of religious duty but also a way to maintain their cultural and spiritual identity.

In particular, family law is an area where Sharia plays a significant role for many Muslims. It offers a distinct set of principles and practices governing marriage, divorce, inheritance, and child custody, among other familial matters. Sharia-driven family law provides a sense of continuity with religious and cultural traditions, offering a framework that is perceived to align with their values and beliefs. It allows individuals to navigate their familial relationships within a framework guided by their understanding of Islamic teachings and norms.

It is important to note that adherence to Sharia-driven practices does not imply a rejection of democracy and liberal freedoms. Muslims who embrace Sharia do not necessarily see it as incompatible with the principles of democratic governance and individual rights. Ghobadzadeh (2014) highlights how, in the case of Iran, the foundations of Sharia provide an Islamic rationale for an inclusive secular democratic state. Sharia, as interpreted by some Muslim scholars, can be seen as offering a moral and ethical framework that can guide the development of laws and institutions in line with democratic principles and human rights.

Similarly, in Turkey, scholars have advocated for a form of secularism that is influenced by Islamic thought and aligns with international conventions of human rights and freedom (Yilmaz 2012). This notion of "Muslim secularism" recognizes the potential compatibility between Islamic values and democratic governance. Proponents of this perspective argue that religious principles can inform a more inclusive, rights-based understanding of secularism, where religious freedom and individual liberties are protected.

Our study looks at the engagement or disengagement of young Muslims living in the West with Sharia-driven thinking. By exploring different categories of Muslim perspectives, we aim to understand the diverse range of thoughts and attitudes within the Muslim community concerning legal pluralism. This exploration considers various factors such as age, ethnicity, migration status/citizenship, educational qualifications, and occupations to ensure a comprehensive representation of the Muslim communities living in the West.

By examining how young Muslims perceive and navigate Sharia-driven practices, we hope to shed light on the complexities and nuances of their experiences. We aim to move beyond simplistic categorizations and stereotypes and provide a more nuanced understanding of how Sharia is understood and applied in the lives of young Muslims in Western societies. Through in-depth interviews and analysis of interviewee perspectives, we can gain insights into the various ways in which Sharia influences identities, values, and decision-making processes.

Furthermore, this study aims to contribute to the broader academic discourse on legal pluralism. It recognizes that formal state laws are not the sole governing mechanisms for individuals and communities. Informal laws, rooted in cultural, religious, and traditional norms, often coexist alongside formal legal systems. Ethnic minorities, in particular, may rely on informal laws when formal laws do not adequately address their specific needs and concerns. This phenomenon of legal pluralism acknowledges the existence of multiple legal orders within a society, each applying to specific situations and social contexts.

By acknowledging the presence of legal pluralism, we can better understand the dynamics of power, authority, and governance within diverse societies. It challenges the notion of a monolithic, state-centred approach to law and recognizes the importance of accommodating diverse identities and cultural practices. Legal pluralism allows for the recognition and validation of different legal mechanisms and traditions, promoting a more inclusive and just society.

1.3 What is Sharia?

Before discussing the details of the book, it is important to understand what is meant by Sharia. The term *Sharia* literally means "path to the watering place" and is commonly expressed in Muslim parlance as the "straight path" to be followed by a believer (Kamali 2008: 2).

Sharia isn't defined by a straightforward set of rules; instead, it draws from a collection of texts that serve as its foundation. These texts, encompassing the

Quran, hadith (Prophetic traditions), and diverse legal writings across various genres, form the authoritative basis for Islamic legal thought and practice. The pursuit among Muslims to understand and implement God's will has historically shaped classical Muslim law. This endeavour to comprehend and enact divine guidance has led to the development and interpretation of legal doctrines drawn from the Quran, hadith, and extensive legal literature, constituting the framework of Islamic jurisprudence (Yilmaz 2016: 32). The *Quran* and *Sunna* are the two most important and primary authorities and sources of Islam. The other instruments referred to as sources are consensus (*ijma*) and analogy (*qiyas*) (Yilmaz 2016: 33). The *Sharia* is derived from the Quran and is understood as divine and immutable law. In Islamic tradition, the Quran holds central importance, being the primary source for the formation of Islamic law. The Sunna, as the second material source of Sharia, follows the Quran in significance. Broadly defined, the Sunna embodies the way of life and actions of the Prophet of Islam in various situations throughout his lifetime. Essentially, the precedents established by the Prophet are encapsulated in the concept of Sunna. The teachings and messages of the Quran were not only interpreted and applied but were also elucidated, embodied, and given practical form through the Sunna of the Prophet. The Sunna serves as a complementary source that helps contextualize and provide practical guidance on implementing the principles outlined in the Quran (Yilmaz 2020: 1).

The distinction between Sharia and fiqh presents a common area of confusion in the literature. Sharia encompasses the entirety of God's commandments, encompassing matters of conduct, belief, and ethics. Fiqh, on the other hand, represents a segment of Sharia. Over time, Muslim scholars have engaged in historical endeavours to understand, discover, and interpret Sharia, resulting in the evolving nature of fiqh, reflecting its human dimension and continuous transformation.

Fiqh, by its nature, remains open to various interpretations and is adaptable according to the circumstances in which it is applied. It tends to be specific and flexible, adapting to the context in which it operates. This adaptability is highlighted by the varying opinions among jurists on specific matters within Islamic law, such as the roles of women in leadership positions or religious practices.

Ijtihad, derived from the root word meaning "striving" or "exerting," is the process of exerting maximum effort by jurists to understand and apply the principles and rules of usūl al-fiqh (legal theory) to discern God's law. It represents an ongoing interpretation and application of Sharia. In situations where explicit text or consensus among scholars is lacking, ijtihad is employed by scholars to interpret and apply Islamic law. However, ijtihad is not permissible in matters already explicitly defined within the Quranic text. Rather, it serves as an effort and process to derive and apply the law from the texts (Quran and Sunna) to specific situations, constituting a case-specific approach rather than a standalone source of law.

Similar to secular law, Islamic law (Sharia) encompasses various facets of social, political, and economic interactions, addressing areas such as marriage, divorce, inheritance, criminal offenses, contracts, commercial transactions, constitutional law, and international law. It parallels secular law in these domains. However, Islamic law uniquely encompasses matters pertaining to individuals' relationships with God, including prayer, fasting, almsgiving, pilgrimage, and other spiritual and ethical concerns (Yilmaz 2020).

Unlike secular law, Islamic law isn't solely enforced by state mechanisms and judges; it also draws its enforcement from the concept of sanctions in the afterlife. This distinction sets it apart significantly from secular law. Additionally, a critical divergence lies in the framework of authority: Islamic law isn't framed by the state but was developed by religious scholars and jurists (ulama) without a centralized governing authority that unifies legal doctrines. This decentralized development distinguishes Islamic law from secular legal systems (Yilmaz 2020).

The interpretive process of Sharia involves ijtihad, denoting human reasoning and intellectual effort in understanding and applying divine laws to real-world situations. This interpretation leads to the development of Islamic jurisprudence, or fiqh, which operates as a dynamic system of laws based on the Quran, Sunna (the practices and teachings of Prophet Muhammad), and hadith (the sayings of the Prophet), alongside various secondary legal sources.

Islamic jurists, known as fuqaha, navigate the complexity of interpreting Sharia by employing diverse methodologies and legal reasoning. These methodologies include ijma (consensus), wherein agreement among scholars holds significant weight in deriving legal rulings, and qiyas (analogical reasoning), which involves applying existing rulings to new situations through logical analogy. Additionally, istihsan (juristic preference) and istislah (consideration of public interest) play roles in accommodating societal changes while adhering to Sharia principles.

The multifaceted nature of Islamic law is evident in the existence of different Sunni legal schools (madhabs), such as Hanafi, Shafi'i, Maliki, and Hanbali, each with distinctive approaches to interpretation and legal rulings. Despite these differences, all madhabs are considered equally valid, contributing to the flexibility and adaptability of fiqh to diverse contexts and needs.

Within the realm of family law, the flexibility and diversity of Islamic legal opinions are evident. For instance, contrasting rulings within different madhabs regarding women's rights to divorce or the practice of polygamy reflect the diverse interpretations and applications of Sharia influenced by cultural, social, and historical contexts.

The debate surrounding secular versus Islamic law often highlights Islamic law's foundation on divine sovereignty. While this holds true, it overlooks the significant role of human agency in the formation of Islamic law. Much like secular law, Islamic law governs civil, social, political, and economic interactions, addressing matters such as marriage, divorce, inheritance, criminal offenses, contracts, commercial transactions, constitutional law, and international law – content that parallels secular law.

However, Islamic law uniquely extends to matters concerning an individual's relationship with God, including practices like prayer, fasting, almsgiving, pilgrimage, and other spiritual matters. This aspect distinguishes Islamic law from secular legal systems.

Unlike Western secular law, which is enforced by state institutions and judges, Sharia is fundamentally upheld by the belief of sanctions in the afterlife, marking a notable difference in enforcement mechanisms. Additionally, Islamic law was not formulated by the state but evolved through the contributions of religious scholars and jurists (ulama), lacking a centralized authority to unify legal doctrine. This decentralized development has resulted in the absence of a singular codified version of Sharia.

Contrary to common assumptions portraying Sharia law as stagnant or outdated, a closer examination reveals the dynamic nature of Islamic legal discourse. Presently, discussions and advancements within Islamic law encompass a wide array of contemporary issues. These include debates on Islamic constitutions, human rights, Sharia-compliant financial transactions and banking, reproductive medical technologies, and other technological matters like the validation of divorce via text message and the recognition of fluctuating digital currencies, among numerous others.

Islamic law showcases its adaptability and responsiveness to evolving circumstances. It remains open to interpretation and adjusts to changing conditions, evidenced by the diversity of topics and developments it addresses. In fact, one could argue that Sharia is currently experiencing a period of heightened vigor and relevance, actively engaging with contemporary issues and demonstrating its resilience and adaptability.

The diversity evident in the contemporary Muslim world is a result of Islam's original message, which later evolved in response to diverse cultural, social, legal, religious, and intellectual contexts. Contrary to the assertion that Islam spread solely through coercion, conversion to Islam was a gradual process. Moreover, Islam did not obliterate local customs and beliefs upon its expansion; rather, it assimilated many of these cultural nuances, incorporating them with an Islamic veneer.

As Islam disseminated, the societies it touched adopted and adapted local cultural, social, and religious elements, shaping their own unique identities within the framework of the Islamic tradition. Despite their variations, each community fashioned its identity based on its interpretation of Islamic teachings. This diversity within the Muslim world highlights the legitimization of various identities, each asserting adherence to the Prophet's message while simultaneously accommodating their distinctive cultural and historical contexts.

As adherents of Islam, Muslims feel an obligation to abide by Islamic law, leading many to strive for a lifestyle that adheres to Sharia principles, even within secular regimes, despite the inherent complexities involved. This commitment prompts many Muslims to navigate the challenges posed by secular legal systems while endeavouring to align their daily lives with the principles and guidance outlined in Islamic law (Yilmaz 2000, 2001, 2016, 2019). Many Muslims, when residing in countries where secular laws align with fundamental Islamic principles, engage in reinterpretation of Islamic law to harmonize it with modern developments (Yilmaz 2023b). This reinterpretation aims to facilitate an Islamic way of life within a secular Western context. This process involves reconciling Islamic teachings with contemporary societal norms and legal frameworks, allowing individuals to navigate their religious practices in accordance with the laws of their country of residence while remaining faithful to their Islamic beliefs.

The field of Islamic jurisprudence or *fiqh* offers Muslim scholars and jurists the opportunity to interpret, elaborate, and contextualize Quranic verses to meet human and context-specific needs. This is helped by a juristic methodology enabling Muslim scholars to use *ijtihad* to reform laws in accordance with time, place, and customary practice. Abdalla (2012: 661) lists a host of secondary legal sources Muslim jurists resort to when deducing legal rulings from the Quran and Sunna. These include *ijma* (consensus), *qiyas* (analogical reasoning), *istihsan* (juristic discretion), *istislah* or *masalah mursala* (consideration of public interest and welfare), *sadd al-dharai* (blocking the means), *istishab* (presumption of continuity), and *urf* (customary practice).

The task of interpreting and deriving Islamic rulings from the Quran and Sunna is primarily assigned to fuqaha (jurists) rather than theologians or philosophers, as acknowledged by most Muslims (Moazam 2011: 317). This recognition highlights the specialized role of legal experts in understanding the ethical and legal implications of Sharia.

Family law serves as a prominent area within Islamic law that illustrates the flexibility in the application of various legal opinions. Different fiqh rulings may appear contradictory or inconsistent but often emerge in response to varying circumstances and methodological considerations. For instance, the Hanafi School of fiqh denies women the right to divorce, whereas the Maliki madhab permits women to seek divorce based on harm (Abu-Odeh 2004: 1072). Similarly, the practice of polygamy diverges between different countries: Tunisia has legally banned polygamy, while Saudi Arabia both allows and legalizes it. In this context, Maurits Berger (2006: 174) draws a comparison between Muslim claims of Sharia-derived laws and the divergent conclusions reached by Dutch and Spanish law, despite drawing from similar legal sources.

These examples demonstrate the dynamic nature of Islamic law and the multiple perspectives that arise within the realm of fiqh. The varying interpretations and legal positions reflect the influence of cultural, social, and historical contexts, as well as the diverse methodologies employed by jurists. Thus, the exercise of legal opinions within Islamic law exemplifies the nuanced approach to navigating the complexities of legal pluralism and the ever-evolving nature of Sharia.

1.4 Added Layer of Diversity

The diversity of Muslims living in the West is another crucial aspect that supports the significance of this study. The term "Muslim community" is often misunderstood in the Western context, as it encompasses a highly diverse group of people with varying ethnic and sectarian backgrounds. Beyond the Sunni and Shia divisions, numerous other sub-sects exist within Islam (Sedgwick 2000). Moreover, it is important to recognize that many Muslims in the West are either migrants or descendants of migrants, which adds another layer of identity based on ethnicity and nationality. Factors such as war, political turmoil, or the pursuit of better opportunities have led and continue to lead Muslims from various continents to seek a new life in the West. This global trend means that Muslim communities in Western countries come from diverse backgrounds.

Furthermore, it is worth noting that within the Western context, a significant number of Caucasians have embraced Islam (Galonnier 2017; Nieuwkerk 2006). In Australia, Islam is one of the fastest-growing religions among Aboriginal communities (Thomas 2016; Onnudottir et al. 2010). Chen and Dorairajoo (2020) found that Dawah activities in the United States were reaching out to Native American communities, and many converts interviewed for their study were drawn to the idea of practicing what is being preached. This overview underscores the increasingly diverse nature of Muslims within various Western countries.

Understanding the diverse backgrounds and experiences of Muslims in the West is essential when examining Islamic legal practice and Sharia debates. The dynamics of cultural, ethnic, and religious diversity shape the perspectives and approaches of Muslims towards Sharia in Western societies. By studying these Muslims, this study aims to provide a comprehensive analysis of the complex interactions between Islamic legal principles, cultural diversity, and the legal frameworks in Western democracies.

This idea of Muslim plurality is central to this book, as it recognizes the immense diversity that exists among Muslims living in the West. Muslims come from various ethnic and sectarian backgrounds, which results in a wide range of interpretations and practices of Sharia. Issues such as prayer times and family law are viewed differently among different ethnic and sectarian groups.

Muslim plurality refers to the wide-ranging diversity and multifaceted nature of Muslim communities, particularly those residing in the Western world. This diversity encompasses a myriad of facets:

1. Ethnic and Cultural Diversity: Muslims in the West hail from various ethnic backgrounds, including Arab, South Asian, African, European, and many others. Each group brings its unique cultural traditions, languages, customs, and historical experiences, contributing to the diversity of Muslim communities.

2. Sectarian Diversity: Within Islam, there are different sects and branches, such as Sunni, Shia, Sufi, and others. Each sect may have distinct beliefs, practices, and interpretations of Islamic teachings, leading to variations in religious rituals, jurisprudence, and religious leadership.
3. Interpretations of Sharia: Sharia, or Islamic law, can be interpreted and applied diversely among different Muslim groups. Matters such as prayer times, dietary practices, dress codes, and family laws may vary based on cultural influences, sect, scholarly interpretations, and individual understandings of religious texts.
4. Social and Economic Diversity: Muslim communities in the West encompass a broad socio-economic spectrum, ranging from affluent professionals to economically marginalized individuals. This diversity influences lifestyle choices, access to resources, educational opportunities, and community dynamics.
5. Geographic Diversity: Muslims in the West come from various geographical regions, contributing to a diverse array of experiences, perspectives, and challenges. This geographic diversity influences how Islam is practiced and integrated into local societies.

Taking a closer look at specific case studies, we can see the extent of this plurality within the Muslim community. Weller and Cheruvallil-Contractor (2014) emphasize the historical context of the UK, which has a history of colonization and significant migration from regions with Muslim populations. As a result, the country has become home to Muslims from all corners of the globe, and the question of "who is a British Muslim?" or "what does it mean to be a Muslim in Britain?" is highly complex. The authors reject the notion of a homogeneous British Muslim identity, highlighting the diverse backgrounds and experiences that shape individuals' understanding of Islam within the British context.

Understanding the diverse and complex nature of the Muslim population in the West is essential for comprehending the dynamics of Islamic legal practice and Sharia debates in this Western context. By exploring the experiences, perspectives, and diverse backgrounds of Western Muslims, this book aims to shed light on the multifaceted nature of Islamic legal engagement within a pluralistic society. It seeks to unravel the various ways in which Muslims navigate their lives between the teachings of Sharia and the legal frameworks of the secular state. By delving into these complexities, the book aims to provide valuable insights into the changing legal landscape and the future of Muslim civil practices in Western democracies.

In Australia, the historical context of the country's immigration policy has shaped the Muslim population and its diversity. The implementation of the "White Australia" policy limited the number of Muslims migrating to Australia, preventing significant migration from communities of colour (Hassan 2015). However, it is important to acknowledge the early contributions of Muslims in Australia, particularly through the "camel transport industry" during the construction of railways, where Afghan workers played a crucial role (Kabir 2005). These early interactions and contributions often go unnoticed or forgotten, such as the participation of Afghan people in the Burke and Wills expedition of 1860–1861, where they served as skilled camel drivers in exploring the challenging terrains of Australia.

The trend of Muslim migration to Australia gained momentum in the 1970s, with significant events like the Soviet invasion of Afghanistan in 1979 leading to an extensive civil war that continued until the invasion of the country in 2001. This conflict resulted in a substantial Afghan community settling in Australia (Kabir 2005). Additionally, during the 1980s and 1990s, waves of migration from Turkey and Lebanon further contributed to the diversity of Muslims in Australia (Hassan 2015). Factors such as war, political instability, and the pursuit of better economic opportunities have attracted Muslims from various parts of the world to migrate to Australia.

Presently, Muslims make up a little over 1% of the total population in Australia. The Muslim community in Australia is not only comprised of individuals from various ethnic backgrounds but also includes a small number of Caucasian Australians, highlighting the heterogeneous mix of Muslims in the country (Alam 2012). Furthermore, it is noteworthy that Islam is the fastest-growing religion among Aboriginal communities, adding yet another layer of diversity to the concept of "Australian Muslims" (Thomas 2016; Onnudottir et al. 2010). Similar to their British counterparts, the identity of Australian Muslims cannot be reduced to a simplistic, two-dimensional portrayal, as it encompasses a wide range of ethnic, cultural, and historical backgrounds.

Understanding the diverse composition of the Muslim population in Australia is vital for comprehending the complexities of Islamic legal practices and the discussions surrounding Sharia in the Australian context. By exploring the experiences and perspectives of Australian Muslims, this book aims to shed light on the multifaceted nature of Islamic legal engagement within the Western context and contribute to the understanding of Muslim civil practices in Western democracies.

In the United States, the Muslim population is characterized by its diverse origins and historical factors. The migrations of Muslims to America were influenced by significant events such as the First World War, which led to uprisings in the Islamic world and subsequent migrations (Hiskett 1993). The Second World War also played a role in Muslim migration to the United States, with migrants coming from India, Pakistan, Eastern Europe, and the Soviet Union (Haddad et al. 1984). These migrations were driven by various reasons, including the search for refuge and the hope of long-term settlement. Many Muslim migrants sought refuge from political or religious oppression, as observed in the case of Palestinian immigrants fleeing religious oppression (Haddad et al. 1984). It is important to note that while some migrants were forced to leave their countries of origin, others migrated voluntarily (Moinuddin 2003). The significant political and economic upheavals pushed many individuals to seek new lives in the United States.

Unlike Australia, the United States did not have a "White only policy," which allowed Muslims to establish a longer-term presence in the country. As a result, Muslim migrants in the United States come from over 60 different backgrounds (Coward et al. 2000). Additionally, when examining the history of the United States, it is essential to acknowledge the significant impact of the slave trade. African slaves forcibly brought to the United States included Muslims among their ranks (Diouf 2021). These early Muslims were enslaved and taken to plantations across the country. Over the twentieth century, there was a wave of conversions to Islam among the African American community, who saw Islam as a means of liberation from racism and slavery (Moinuddin 2003). Islam represented something new and offered an alternative to their life of oppression. Outside of prison, Islam gained popularity among African Americans as a form of resistance against discrimination in the United States. The African American Muslim community emphasized the importance of race and ethnicity not dividing Muslims (McCloud 2003: 161). Prominent leaders like Malcolm X spoke about the racial dynamics within American society, critiquing white churches for promoting white nationalism (Malcolm 1964).

Considering the diverse backgrounds and historical experiences of Muslims in the United States, it becomes evident that the concept of "American Muslims" is multifaceted and cannot be reduced to a single narrative. This diversity influences the understanding and practice of Islam within the American context and highlights the need to explore the various perspectives and experiences of Muslims living in the United States. By examining the dynamics of Islamic legal engagement and the intersection of Sharia with American society, this book aims to contribute to a comprehensive understanding of Muslim civil practices in Western democracies.

In the United States, the number of Caucasian converts to Islam is growing, adding to the diversity of the Muslim population (Chouhoud 2021). Among the American Muslim converts, a significant portion consists of women. In the past, many female conversions were a result of marriage to a Muslim husband (Bowen 2009; Anway 2000). However, over time, more women began converting to Islam independently, driven by personal engagements with Islam through college friends, Muslim neighbours, travels to Muslim countries, or independent research (Anway 2000; Kose 2010). The increasing visibility of Islam and Muslims in America exposed more people to the religion and its rituals, leading them to learn about Islam and inspiring them to convert through interactions with Muslims (Anway 2000).

Regarding the Muslim groups in America, as mentioned earlier, Muslim Americans belong to a wide range of groups and schools of thought. They are divided based on their ethnic origin, leaders, or denominations. Many of these groups found refuge in America for their beliefs, even if they faced persecution in their home countries. The Ahmadiyya Muslim Community is believed to be the oldest Muslim community in the United States, appealing to various racial and ethnic groups and utilizing the impact of racial discrimination to attract new followers (Turner 2003). African Americans founded several organizations that experienced significant growth, such as the Nation of Islam (NOI), while others, like the Moorish Science Temple, the Five Percenters, and the United Nations of Islam, declined over time (Allen 2000; Paghdiwala 2007).

While three-quarters of Muslims in the United States are migrants, a portion of the population was born in the country or converted to the faith. However, it is important to note that White Muslims constitute less than 1% of the estimated 3.45 million Muslims living in the United States (Pew 2017).

Overall, as observed in all three case studies (see also in detail, Yilmaz 2023a), there is no singular type of "Muslims" in Western countries. The heterogeneity within Muslim communities highlights the plural interpretations of Sharia and its varied applications among different groups. The diverse backgrounds, ethnicities, and experiences of Muslims contribute to the dynamic landscape of Islamic legal practice in Western societies.

1.5 Methodology

This book employs a comprehensive qualitative approach to understand the multifaceted experiences of young Muslims living in Western countries. By adopting a qualitative methodology, the study aims to provide a nuanced understanding of the participants' beliefs, practices, and engagements within their respective societies. This approach enables the exploration of their lived realities, shedding light on the diverse ways in which they navigate their religious identities and negotiate their place in Western societies.

In line with existing scholarly works in the field, this research draws upon the rich tradition of detailed interviews to investigate the multifaceted aspects of the lives of young Muslims (Nilsson 2022; De Nolf et al. 2021; Younis & Hassan 2019; Selby 2016; Harris & Roose 2014; Barkdull et al. 2011). Through these in-depth interviews, the study aims to capture the lived experiences, perspectives, and challenges faced by young Muslims in Western societies. This approach allows for a deeper exploration of their thoughts, emotions, and motivations, giving voice to their individual narratives and countering common misconceptions and stereotypes.

Qualitative research methods provide a platform for understanding the complexities of the young Muslim experience. By focussing on the rich and diverse narratives of the participants, this study aims to transcend surface-level generalizations and stereotypes, revealing the unique stories, struggles, and triumphs of these individuals. Through open-ended interviews, the researchers seek to foster a supportive and inclusive environment that encourages participants to share their perspectives and personal journeys, resulting in a more comprehensive and authentic portrayal of their experiences.

Moreover, qualitative research allows for the identification and exploration of emergent themes and patterns that may not have been initially anticipated. By employing a thematic analysis approach, the researchers can identify recurring ideas, beliefs, and practices that shape the lives of young Muslims. This process involves coding and categorizing the data, drawing connections between different elements, and uncovering underlying meanings and interpretations. Through this inductive approach, the study aims to generate rich and nuanced findings that capture the complexity and diversity of the young Muslim experience in the Western context.

The interview questions were carefully designed to explore a wide range of themes and perspectives relevant to the experiences of young Muslims in Western societies. The topics covered in the questions included voting behaviour, social engagement, political participation, and knowledge of Islamic law (Sharia). The aim was to capture the participants' thoughts, beliefs, and experiences related to these aspects, providing insights into their engagement with the broader society and their understanding of their religious and cultural identities.

The interview questions were open-ended, encouraging the participants to provide detailed and personal responses. For example, participants were asked to describe how they perceive their own identity, share their thoughts on the role of Muslims in politics, and discuss their experiences of participating in civil protests. The questionnaire also covered topics such as religious identity, familiarity with Islamic law, and the relevance of Sharia outside of Muslim-majority countries. These questions aimed to explore the participants' beliefs, values, and engagement with their faith and the wider society.

A total of 122 participants,[1] aged between 18 and 24 years, were interviewed for this study. These participants were residents of three English-speaking Western countries: Australia, the United States, and the United Kingdom at the time of the interviews. They were either born in these countries, moved there at a young age, or were temporary residents at the time of the survey. The sampling process was conducted by three local research assistants (RAs) who used convenience sampling to approach potential participants. However, the RAs considered demographic variables such as gender, ethnicity, religion (including different sects), and occupation to ensure a representative sample.

The selection of Australia, the United Kingdom, and the United States for the study was based on the large Muslim populations in these countries and their representation of different continents. Recent statistics indicate that approximately 2.6% of the population in Australia, 7% in the United Kingdom, and 1.1% in the United States identify as Muslim (Office of National Statistics 2019; Australian Bureau of Statistics 2017).

The sample of 122 participants was diverse in terms of ethnicity, but all identified as Muslims. The breakdown of participants by country was as follows: Australia (64), the United States (30), and the United Kingdom (28). The majority of participants were born in their respective Western countries, with a small portion being non-citizens.

The interviews were conducted in English and recorded for later transcription. A professional transcriber transcribed the audio recordings into text format. Due to the COVID-19 pandemic, some interviews were conducted in

1 Please see Table 1.0 in the Appendix for details on participants' demographics.

person, while others were carried out remotely using platforms such as Skype, Zoom, or Messenger. Participants were given the flexibility to choose the time and place for in-person interviews to minimize inconvenience. Prior to the interviews, the participants received an introduction to the research background and were provided with a consent form, which they signed to indicate their agreement to participate. Additionally, participants completed a closed-ended survey before the interviews commenced, which was returned to the researcher. To ensure participant anonymity, pseudonyms based on the participants' ethnicity and gender were used when presenting quotations from the interviews, capturing the context and essence of the participants' statements.

The interviews conducted for this study spanned a significant period, from mid-2018 to 2020, capturing a wide range of participant experiences and perspectives. The immediate transcription of the interviews by a professional transcriber ensured that the rich data collected was preserved in written form. To further enhance the reliability and accuracy of the transcriptions, a second transcriber authenticated the initial scripts, adding an additional layer of quality control to the process. This meticulous approach to transcription laid the groundwork for the subsequent analysis.

Data analysis played a crucial role in studying the intricacies of the participants' narratives. The analysis process involved coding, which entailed systematically categorizing and organizing the data into coherent themes (Bryman 2001). Both deductive (priori) and inductive coding methods were employed to capture a comprehensive understanding of the data. The initial codes were driven by the existing literature on the topic, providing a theoretical foundation for the analysis. However, the flexibility of the inductive coding approach allowed for the discovery of new themes and insights that emerged directly from the participants' voices (Ryan & Bernard 2003).

Within the participants' accounts, several key themes emerged, shedding light on their understanding of Islam, particularly in relation to the concept of Sharia. The participants' perspectives on the use and relevance of Sharia in their lives were explored in depth. This encompassed discussions on how Sharia functions within Muslim-majority countries, as well as its perceived significance in non-Muslim majority societies. The role of digital technology in religious practices also emerged as a prominent theme, illustrating how young Muslims navigate the intersection of faith and modernity.

Furthermore, the participants' relationships with imams, as well as the influence of religion on their political and civil participation, were integral aspects of the study. The participants' insights into their interactions with religious leaders provided valuable insights into how imams shape their understanding and application of Islamic principles. Moreover, the examination of how religion influences their engagement with political and civil activities sheds light on the multifaceted nature of their identities as both Muslims and active members of Western societies.

Drawing from the extensive data analysis, this book is structured around the identified themes and subthemes, allowing for a comprehensive exploration of how informal law, often referred to as legal pluralism, impacts the worldviews and practices of young Muslims residing in Western countries. By delving into the lived experiences of these individuals, the book aims to provide a nuanced understanding of the complex dynamics between religious beliefs, legal frameworks, and the broader social context.

The rigorous data analysis process employed in this study, including transcription, coding, and theme identification, has laid the foundation for an in-depth exploration of the experiences and perspectives of young Muslims living in the West. The book utilizes the rich narratives of the participants to shed light on the role of informal law and its influence on their identities, beliefs, and societal engagement.

1.6 Layout of the Book

This book is based on eight chapters in total. Chapter 1 serves as the introductory chapter of the book, setting the stage for the subsequent chapters. It begins by outlining the aims and objectives of the book, which include exploring the understanding and impact of Sharia on the lives of young Muslims in Australia, the United States, and the United Kingdom. The chapter highlights the significance of this research by emphasizing the diversity within Muslim thought regarding Sharia and its relevance in the lives of Muslims living as minorities in Western countries. The chapter provides a detailed overview of the methodology employed in the study. It explains the rationale behind using a qualitative approach, specifically in-depth interviews, to gather data from the participants. The use of semi-structured questions and the process of data collection are described, including the considerations taken into account during sampling to ensure a representative sample of young Muslims in the three case study countries. Furthermore, the chapter establishes the need for this book by discussing the demographic compositions of Muslims living in Australia, the United States, and the United Kingdom. It highlights the presence of Muslims as a significant and diverse population within these Western countries, with different ethnic backgrounds, migration statuses, and levels of religious practice. The chapter also sheds light on the role of informal laws, such as Sharia, in the lives of Muslims living as minorities in Western countries. It emphasizes that informal laws have become an integral part of the lives of many Muslims, shaping their perspectives, behaviours, and aspirations. The chapter underscores the importance of studying how young Muslims navigate the interaction between informal laws and the formal legal systems of the countries they reside in. In summary, Chapter 1 introduces the book by outlining its aims, objectives, and methodology. It highlights the diversity within Muslim thought, the demographic compositions of Muslims in the three-case study countries, and the significance of informal laws in the lives of Muslims living as minorities in Western countries. This chapter sets the foundation for the subsequent chapters, which look at specific themes and findings related to the understanding and impact of Sharia on young Muslims in the West.

Chapter 2 discusses the presence and influence of informal laws driven by Sharia, the Islamic legal framework, among Western Muslims. Informal laws exist outside the formal legal framework and are shaped by religious beliefs and practices governing various aspects of life, such as inheritance, marriage, dietary choices, celebrations, and banking practices. This study examines the typology of informal laws, drawing from Helmke and Levitsky, which categorizes them into competing, substitutive, complementary, and accommodating types. The clash between informal and formal legal systems arises from the informality of the former and the uniformity of the latter. State laws often fail to accommodate parallel opinions on personal and collective matters, prompting the emergence of informal laws as alternative systems to address the diverse needs of different groups. Within the realm of informal laws, there is a recognition of plurality influenced by theological differences among subsects of Islam. For instance, the practice of temporary marriage sparks debates among different sectarian groups. Sharia-driven informal laws extend beyond legal issues, governing all aspects of life, including matters of protocol and etiquette. However, the acceptance and integration of Sharia-driven informal laws within Western legal systems and societies face challenges. The United Kingdom, with its significant Muslim population, experiences ongoing debates regarding the use of Sharia law in family law and arbitration. Concerns arise about potential conflicts with human rights charters and the impact on women's rights, especially in cases involving polygamy. This chapter aims to provide insights into the presence and significance of Sharia-driven informal laws among Western Muslims, shedding light on legal pluralism and its implications. By examining the typology, manifestations, and debates surrounding these laws, this study contributes to a comprehensive understanding of the complex dynamics within Western legal systems and societies.

Chapter 3 focusses on exploring the themes of connection with faith among the young Muslims interviewed in the study. It analyzes the multifaceted nature of their religious identity and how it is influenced by a range of factors. One key aspect discussed in this chapter is the role of family in shaping their connection with faith. Many participants expressed that their religious beliefs and practices were instilled in them from a young age by their parents or immediate family members. They describe how their upbringing and the teachings they received at home have influenced their understanding and practice of Islam. Additionally, the chapter examines the impact of the Muslim community on their faith. Participants who had regular interaction with the community through activities at the mosque, religious events, and social gatherings often reported a stronger sense of connection to their faith. They find support, guidance, and a sense of belonging within the community, which reinforces their religious identity. The chapter also highlights the role of personal experiences and societal influences in shaping participants' understanding and practice of Islam. Participants reflect on how their experiences, both positive and negative, have impacted their faith. They also discuss the influence of broader societal factors, such as media portrayals or public perceptions of

Islam, on their relationship with their faith. Overall, this chapter provides a comprehensive exploration of the diverse range of experiences and perspectives regarding faith among the participants. It examines the complex interplay of family, community, personal experiences, and societal influences in shaping their connection with Islam. Through these insights, the chapter contributes to a deeper understanding of the multifaceted nature of religious identity among young Muslims in the study.

Chapter 4 provides an analysis of the typologies of young Muslims based on their views on Sharia, offering a comprehensive analysis of their perspectives and beliefs. The chapter identifies two primary typologies: The Legal Pluralists and the Muslim Secularists (Yilmaz 2023b), with further exploration of sub-types within each category. The Legal Pluralists are young Muslims who advocate for the coexistence of Sharia and existing legal systems in Western countries, considering legal pluralism as a viable approach. In contrast, the Muslim Secularists hold a more secular worldview and perceive Sharia as having limited relevance in their lives. The chapter presents these typologies and sub-types by conducting an in-depth analysis of the participants' attitudes, perspectives, and beliefs towards Sharia. It sheds light on the complexities and nuances within the Muslim community, showcasing the diverse range of views on Sharia. The analysis highlights the intricate relationship between faith, culture, and legal systems, revealing the diversity of opinions and understandings regarding the role of Sharia. By exploring the themes related to faith and views on Sharia, the chapter provides a comprehensive understanding of how young Muslims in the West connect with their faith and perceive the significance of Sharia in their lives. It presents a rich variety of experiences, beliefs, and perspectives, demonstrating the multiplicity of voices within the Muslim community. The chapter concludes by emphasizing the need to recognize the varied views among Muslims regarding Sharia, setting the stage for further exploration in subsequent chapters. Overall, this chapter contributes to a nuanced understanding of the diverse range of perspectives on Sharia among young Muslims, illustrating the complexities surrounding their beliefs and attitudes. It adds depth to the analysis of faith and its intersection with legal systems, highlighting the heterogeneity within the Muslim community and laying the groundwork for further examination in the following chapters.

Chapter 5 studies the relationship between young Muslims and imams, focussing on the role of imams as a source of Sharia and religious guidance. The chapter explores various themes that shed light on why young Muslims seek the help of an imam or choose to avoid them altogether. One of the key areas of exploration is the factors influencing young Muslims' decision to approach an imam. The chapter examines how factors such as gender, ethnicity, and sectarian considerations play a role in determining which imam participants turn to for religious guidance. It explores the dynamics of seeking advice and support from imams who share similar backgrounds and experiences, as well as the challenges and considerations involved in seeking guidance from imams of different backgrounds. The chapter also focusses on the expectations and preferences of young Muslims when choosing an imam. It explores the qualities and attributes that young Muslims value in an imam, including their knowledge, approachability, relatability, and ability to address contemporary issues. It discusses the importance of finding an imam who can provide relevant guidance within the context of their lives as young Muslims living in the West. Through the examination of these themes, the chapter offers insights into the complex dynamics of the relationship between young Muslims and imams. It highlights the diverse factors influencing their decisions and the nuanced considerations involved in seeking religious guidance. The chapter provides a deeper understanding of how young Muslims navigate their relationship with imams and the significance of this relationship in shaping their understanding and practice of Sharia. By exploring the multifaceted aspects of the relationship between young Muslims and imams, the chapter contributes to the broader understanding of how informal sources of Sharia influence the lives of young Muslims in the West. It sheds light on the role of imams as a source of religious knowledge and guidance and the impact of this relationship on the participants' perspectives and engagement with Sharia.

Chapter 6 analyzes the growing relevance of online spaces for young Muslims and their engagement with digital platforms. It introduces the concept of "Sheikh Google," a term used to capture the reliance of young Muslims on the internet as a source of information and religious guidance. The chapter explores the multifaceted nature of young Muslims' interaction with online spaces, highlighting both the benefits and challenges associated with this trend. One of the key themes explored in this chapter is the use of the internet as a platform for seeking religious information. It examines how young Muslims turn to online sources, such as websites, forums, and social media platforms, to find answers to their questions about Islam and Sharia. The chapter investigates the motivations behind this reliance on online platforms, including the accessibility, convenience, and diversity of information available. While online spaces provide a wealth of information, the chapter also addresses the reservations and concerns that young Muslims may have regarding the authenticity and reliability of online sources. It explores the challenges of verifying information and the potential risks of misinformation or misinterpretation. The chapter discusses how young Muslims navigate these concerns and develop critical thinking skills to discern reliable sources of knowledge online. Furthermore, the chapter examines the emergence of "influencer imams" on social media platforms. It explores the role of these influential figures who use digital platforms to disseminate religious teachings, provide guidance, and engage with young Muslims. The chapter discusses the impact of influencer imams on shaping young Muslims' perspectives, practices, and understanding of Sharia. Lastly, the chapter investigates how young Muslims perceive online spaces as platforms for showcasing the positive aspects of Islam and earning "good deeds" (hasanat). It explores how young Muslims use online platforms to promote Islamic values, share positive stories, and counter negative stereotypes about Islam and Muslims. It also examines the motivations behind these activities and the potential impact they have on young Muslims' engagement with their faith and the wider society. Through the exploration of these themes, the chapter sheds light on the complex relationship between young Muslims and online spaces. It highlights the opportunities and challenges presented by digital platforms in shaping their understanding of Sharia and their engagement with Islamic teachings. The chapter provides insights into how young Muslims navigate the online world, seeking knowledge, engaging with influencer imams, and using online spaces to promote a positive image of Islam.

Chapter 7 explores the extent to which Sharia influences the civic participation of young Muslims. This chapter is divided into subthemes that explore the relationship between Sharia and voting, running for office, and engaging in protests. It also examines the role of imams as a source of Sharia-driven thinking on these civic issues. The first subtheme focusses on voting and explores how Sharia shapes young Muslims' perspectives on political participation. It investigates their understanding of the importance of voting as a civic duty and how Islamic teachings influence their decision to participate in the democratic process. The chapter examines how young Muslims reconcile their religious beliefs and values with the political systems in which they reside. The second subtheme centres around running for office and examines the aspirations of young Muslims to hold positions of political leadership. It explores how Sharia influences their motivations and aspirations for political representation. The chapter investigates whether young Muslims perceive political leadership as a means to promote Islamic values and contribute to the betterment of society according to their understanding of Sharia. The third subtheme focusses on protesting and explores the role of Sharia in shaping young Muslims' engagement in social and political activism. It investigates whether and how Sharia-based principles influence their decision to participate in protests and demonstrations. The chapter examines the intersection between religious beliefs, social justice, and activism, shedding light on the motivations behind young Muslims' involvement in protest movements. Throughout these subthemes, the chapter also addresses the role of imams as a source of Sharia-driven thinking on civic participation issues. It investigates the frequency and nature of consultations young Muslims have with imams regarding voting, running for office, and engaging in protests. The chapter explores the extent to which imams provide guidance and religious interpretations that shape young Muslims' views and actions in the civic sphere. By exploring these themes, the chapter provides insights into the ways in which Sharia influences the civic participation of young Muslims. It sheds light on their perspectives on voting, running for office, and protesting and examines how their engagement with imams informs their understanding and decision-making in these areas. The chapter contributes to a broader understanding of the relationship between Sharia and civic participation among young Muslims in Western societies.

Chapter 8 serves as the conclusion of the book, bringing together the key findings from the previous chapters and offering a comprehensive discussion of the research findings. The chapter begins by summarizing the main themes and insights that emerged from the analysis of the data. It highlights the diverse perspectives and experiences of young Muslims living in the West regarding Sharia and its influence on various aspects of their lives. The chapter emphasizes the importance of understanding the multifaceted nature of Sharia and its role in shaping the beliefs, behaviours, and civic participation of young Muslims. Furthermore, the conclusion chapter reflects on the implications of the findings for broader society. It addresses the significance of recognizing the agency and individual interpretations of Sharia among young Muslims, challenging stereotypes and misconceptions that often prevail. It emphasizes the importance of fostering an inclusive and pluralistic society that respects the religious freedom and diverse perspectives of Muslim communities. In addition to summarizing the key findings, the chapter also discusses the limitations of the study and identifies potential avenues for future research. It acknowledges that the study focussed on a specific age group and three Western countries and suggests that future research could explore different age groups, regions, and cultural contexts to enhance further our understanding of the relationship between young Muslims and Sharia. The chapter concludes with a call for continued research on the topic, highlighting the need for longitudinal studies to examine how young Muslims' perspectives and experiences evolve over time. It also encourages interdisciplinary approaches that combine sociological, psychological, and legal perspectives to provide a comprehensive understanding of the complex dynamics at play. Overall, the conclusion chapter provides a comprehensive synthesis of the key findings and their implications while also paving the way for future research directions in the field. By doing so, it contributes to ongoing scholarly discussions and promotes a deeper understanding of the lived experiences and perspectives of young Muslims in relation to Sharia in Western societies.

References

Abdalla, Mohamad. 2012. "Sacred Law in a Secular Land: To What Extent Should Sharī 'a Law be Followed in Australia?" *Griffith Law Review*, 21(3): 657–679.

Abu-Odeh, Lama. 2004. "Modernizing Muslim Family Law: The Case of Egypt." *Vanderbilt Journal of Transnational Law*, 37: 1043–1146.

Alam, O., 2012. "'Islam is a Blackfella Religion, Whatchya Trying to Prove?': Race in the Lives of White Muslim Converts in Australia." *The La Trobe Journal*, 89: 124–139.

Anway, Carol L. 2000. "American Women Choosing Islam." In *Muslims on the Americanization Path?* edited by Yvonne Yazbeck Haddad and John L. Esposito. New York: Oxford University Press, 145–160.

Australian Bureau of Statistics. 2017. *Census of Population and Housing: Reflecting Australia – Stories from the Census, 2016.* Accessed 7 May 2021. www.abs.gov.au/AUSSTATS/abs@.nsf/DetailsPage/2071.02016?OpenDocument

Barkdull, C., Khaja, K., Queiro-Tajalli, I., Swart, A., Cunningham, D. and Dennis, S. 2011. "Experiences of Muslims in four Western countries post 9/11." *Affilia*, 26(2): 139–153.

Berger M. 2006. "Sharia Law in Canada – Also Possible in the Netherlands?'" In *Crossing Borders: Essays in European and Private International Law, Nationality Law, and Islamic Law in Honour of Frans Van Der Velden*, edited by P van Der Grinten and T Heukels. Alphen aan den Rijn: Kluwer.

Bowen, Patrick D. 2009. "Conversion to Islam in the United States: A Case Study in Denver, Colorado." *International West Journal of Religious Studies*, 1(1): 41–64.

Bryman, A. 2001. *Social Research Methods.* Oxford and New York: Oxford University Press.

Chen, Y. and Dorairajoo, S. 2020. "American Muslims' Da'wah Work and Islamic Conversion." *Religions*, 11(8): 383. www.mdpi.com/778166

Chouhoud, Youssef. 2021. *Who are White Muslims?* ISPU. 30 April. Accessed 2 April 2023. www.ispu.org/who-are-white-muslims/

Coward, Harold, Hinnells, John R. and Williams, Raymond Brady, eds. 2000. *The South Asian Religious Diaspora in Britain, Canada, and the United States.* Albany: State University of New York Press.

De Nolf, Ans, d'Haenens, Leen and Mekki-Berrada, Abdelwahed. 2021. "Face to Face with Anti-Muslim Sentiment: A Qualitative Study into the Coping Mechanisms of Young College and University Muslim Students and Graduates in Flanders." *Religions*, 12(2): 135.

Diouf, Sylviane A. 2021. "Muslims in America: A Forgotten History." *Al Jazeera*. 10 February. Accessed 2 April 2023. www.aljazeera.com/features/2021/2/10/muslims-in-america-always-there

Galonnier, J. 2017. *Choosing Faith and Facing Race: Converting to Islam in France and the United States.* Northwestern University. https://search.proquest.com/openview/4a79913c10d18723fff3e7600052fc76/1?pq-origsite=gscholar&cbl=18750

Ghobadzadeh, Naser. 2014. *Religious Secularity: A Theological Challenge to the Islamic State.* Oxford and New York: Oxford University Press.

Griffiths, John. 1986. "What is Legal Pluralism?" *The Journal of Legal Pluralism and Unofficial Law*, 18: 1–55.

Haddad, Yvonne Yazbeck, Haines, Byron and Findly Ellison, eds. 1984. *The Islamic Impact.* Syracuse: Syracuse University Press.

Harris, A. and Roose, J. 2014. "DIY Citizenship Amongst Young Muslims: Experiences of the 'Ordinary'." *Journal of Youth Studies*, 17(6): 794–813.

Hassan, R. 2015. *Australian Muslims: A Demographic, Social and Economic Profile of Muslims in Australia.* International Centre for Muslim and non-Muslim Understanding. https://apo.org.au/node/56353

Hiskett, Mervyn. 1993. *Some to Mecca Tum to Pray: Islamic Values and the Modem World.* London: Claridge Press.

Hoffman, Murad. 1993. *Islam: The Alternative.* Reading: Garnet Publishing.

Kabir, N. A. 2005. "The Economic Plight of the Afghans in Australia. 1860–2000." *Islamic Studies*, 44(2): 229–250. www.jstor.org/stable/20838963

Kamali, Mohammad Hashim. 2008. *Shariah Law: An Introduction.* Oxford: One world Publications.

Kose, Ali. 2010. *Conversion to Islam: A Study of Native British Converts.* Abingdon: Routledge.

Malcolm X. 1964. "The Ballot or the Bullet". *Speech Delivered in Detroit (USA).* 12 April. Accessed 2 August 2018. http://americanradioworks.publicradio.org/features/blackspeech/mx.html

McCloud, Aminah Beverly. 2003. "Islam in America: The Mosaic." In *Religion and immigration: Christian, Jewish, and Muslim experiences in the United States.* New York: Altamira Press, 159–174.

Moazam, Farhat. 2011. "Sharia Law and Organ Transplantation: Through the Lens of Muslim Jurists." *Asian Bioethics Review*, 3(4): 316–332.

Moinuddin, Iffat Mohammadi. 2003. *Muslim Migration into the US: A Study of the Motivations and Consequences behind Migration and Settlement Patterns*. Chancellor's Honors Program Projects. https://trace.tennessee.edu/utk_chanhonoproj/670

Nieuwkerk, K. V. 2006. "Introduction. Gender and conversion to Islam in the West." In *Women Embracing Islam: Gender and Conversion in the West*. University of Texas Press, 1–16. www.degruyter.com/document/doi/10.7560/712737-003/html

Nilsson, Marco. 2022. "Motivations for Jihad and Cognitive Dissonance – A Qualitative Analysis of Former Swedish Jihadists." *Studies in Conflict & Terrorism*, 45(1): 92–110.

Office of National Statistics. 2019. *Population Estimates*. www.ons.gov.uk/peoplepopulationandcommunity/populationandmigration/populationestimates#:~:text=The%20UK%20population%20was%20estimated,the%20year%20to%20mid%2D2018.

Onnudottir, H., Possamai, A. and Turner, B. 2010. "Islam: A New Religious Vehicle for Aboriginal Self-Empowerment in Australia?" *International Journal for the Study of New Religions*, 1(1): 49–73. https://journal.equinoxpub.com/IJSNR/article/view/12211

Paghdiwala, Tasneem. 2007. "The Aging of the Moors." *Chicago Reader*. November 15. Accessed 28 September. www.chicagoreader.com/chicago/the-aging-of-the-moors/Content?oid=999633

Pew. 2017. *U.S. Muslims Concerned About Their Place in Society, But Continue to Believe in The American Dream*. Pew Research Centre. 26 July. Accessed 2 April 2022. www.pewresearch.org/religion/2017/07/26/demographic-portrait-of-muslim-americans/

Ryan, W. Gery and Bernard, H. Russell. 2003. "Techniques to Identify Themes." *Field Methods*, 15(1).

Sedgwick, M. 2000. "Sects in the Islamic World1." *Nova Religio: The Journal of Alternative and Emergent Religions*, 3(2): 195–240. https://doi.org/10.1525/nr.2000.3.2.195

Selby, Jennifer A. 2016. ""Muslimness" and Multiplicity in Qualitative Research and in Government Reports in Canada." *Critical Research on Religion*, 4(1): 72–89.

Thomas, Jason. 2016. "What's the Fastest Growing Religion in Australia?" *SBS News*. 15 September. Accessed 2 April 2023. www.sbs.com.au/news/article/whats-the-fastest-growing-religion-in-australia/1uwk4w2ld

Turner, Richard Brent. 2003. *Islam in the African American Experience*. Bloomington, Indianapolis: Indiana University Press.

Vanderlinden, Jacques. 1971. "Le pluralisme juridique: Essai de synthese." In *Le pluralisme juridique*, edited by John Gilissen. Brussels: Université de Bruxelles, 19–56.

Weller, P. and Cheruvallil-Contractor, S. 2014. "Muslims in the UK." In *After integration: Islam, Conviviality and Contentious Politics in Europe*, edited by Marian Burchardt and Ines Michalowski. Wiesbaden: Springer Fachmedien Wiesbaden, 303–325.

Yilmaz, Ihsan. 2000. "Muslim Law in Britain, Reflections in the Socio-Legal Sphere and Differential Legal Treatment." *Journal of Muslim Minority Affairs*, 20(2): 353–360. https://doi.org/10.1080/713680357

Yilmaz, Ihsan. 2001. "Law as Chameleon: The Question of Incorporation of Muslim Personal Law into the English Law." *Journal of Muslim Minority Affairs*, 21(2): 297–308.

Yilmaz, Ihsan. 2002. "The Challenge of Post-Modern Legality and Muslim Legal Pluralism in England." *Journal of Ethnic and Migration Studies*, 28(2): 343–354.

Yilmaz, Ihsan. 2012. "Towards a Muslim Secularism? An Islamic 'Twin Tolerations' Understanding of Religion in the Public Sphere." *Turkish Journal of Politics*, 3(2): 41–52.

Yilmaz, Ihsan. 2016. *Muslim Laws, Politics and Society in Modern Nation States: Dynamic Legal Pluralisms in England, Turkey and Pakistan*. London and New York: Routledge.

Yilmaz, Ihsan. 2019. "Nation Building, Islamic Law and Unofficial Legal Pluralism: The Cases of Turkey and Pakistan." In *Legal Legal Pluralism in Muslim Contexts*, edited by Norbert Oberauer, Yvonne Prief and Ulrike Qubaja. Leiden, The Netherlands: Brill, 109–138.

Yilmaz, Ihsan. 2020. "Muslims, Sacred Texts, and Laws in the Modern World." In *Handbook of Contemporary Islam and Muslim Lives*, edited by M. Woodward and R. Lukens-Bull. Cham: Springer, 1–18.

Yilmaz, Ihsan. 2022. *Authoritarianism, Informal Law, and Legal Hybridity: The Islamisation of the State in Turkey*. Singapore: Palgrave Macmillan.

Yilmaz, Ihsan. 2023a. *Islam in the Anglosphere: Perspectives of Young Muslims in Australia, the UK and the USA*. Singapore: Palgrave Macmillan.

Yilmaz, Ihsan. 2023b. "Muslim Secularism by Conduct: Attitudes of Young Australian Muslims to Legal Pluralism and Sharia." *Journal of Intercultural Studies*, 44(2): 274–288. https://doi.org/10.1080/07256868.2022.2104826

Younis, Tarek and Hassan, Ghayda. 2019. "Second-Generation Western Muslims: A Qualitative Analysis of Multiple Social Identities." *Transcultural Psychiatry*, 56(6): 1155–1169.

2 Sharia as Informal Law in the Lives of Western Muslims

2.1 Introduction

The chapter discusses the presence of informal laws influenced by Sharia among Western Muslims. The conflict between informal and formal legal systems arises from the informal nature of the former and the rigid uniformity of the latter. The rigid framework of state-supported formal laws often fails to accommodate divergent perspectives on personal and collective issues, prompting the emergence of informal legal structures as alternative systems. While state laws tend to be standardized and may not sufficiently address diverse opinions on personal and collective matters, informal legal systems, including those rooted in Sharia, have emerged or have continued to coexist as alternatives. These informal systems highlight the limitations of formal laws in meeting the varied needs of different groups.

The chapter highlights the prevalence of Sharia-influenced informal laws among Western Muslims, governing an array of life aspects, including inheritance, marriage, dietary preferences, celebrations, and financial practices. Recognizing the diverse subsects within Islam, it acknowledges varying perspectives on religious practices and political issues. Debates within different sectarian groups, such as on temporary marriage, exemplify this diversity.

These informal laws, rooted in Sharia, are positioned as competitors to formal state laws, offering alternative viewpoints and addressing the varied needs of distinct groups. Their existence underscores their pervasive role in governing various life domains, encompassing not only legal matters but also aspects of etiquette and protocol.

These informal laws encompass various aspects of life, such as inheritance, marriage, dietary choices, celebrations, and banking practices. Unlike formal legal frameworks, informal laws are shaped by religious beliefs and operate outside official systems. Within the realm of informal law, there exists a plurality of views due to theological differences among different subsects of Islam. Overall, the chapter highlights the complex dynamics surrounding the existence and acceptance of Sharia-driven informal laws in Western countries, showcasing the various challenges and debates surrounding their role within legal systems and society.

DOI: 10.4324/9781003482604-2

2.2 Informal Institutions

An institution, in the realm of social and political analysis, can be understood as a "regularized pattern of interaction that is known, practiced, and accepted (if not necessarily approved) by actors who expect to continue interacting under the rules sanctioned and backed by that pattern" (O'Donnell, 1996, 34). Within this context, the study of informal institutions and informal politics has garnered increasing attention and significance (Lauth, 2000).

Building upon this foundation, Helmke and Levitsky (2004, 727) provide a concise definition of informal institutions as "socially shared rules, usually unwritten, that are created, communicated, and enforced outside of officially sanctioned channels." These informal institutions arise as a response to the needs and aspirations of social groups that may feel alienated or excluded from formal political structures. In such cases, these groups organize themselves within alternative political structures that operate alongside, or even in contrast to, the established formal institutions. This phenomenon highlights the existence of parallel systems of governance that influence societal behaviour, decision-making processes, and power dynamics.

Over the years, various studies have shed light on the significance of unwritten rules and informal institutions in understanding the dynamics of societies. The emergence of concepts such as "prismatic societies," "moral economies," "economies of affection," legal pluralism, clientelism, corruption, and consociationalism has underscored the central role played by informal institutions in shaping societal behaviour and governance (Helmke and Levitsky, 2004, 725). These concepts draw attention to the informal practices, norms, and networks that operate within societies, often outside the purview of formal state institutions.

Informal institutions encompass a wide range of phenomena, including local customs, reputations, and what can be described as "folkways." Though not codified in official statutes or regulations, these informal practices and norms exert a considerable influence on the behaviour and interactions of individuals and groups within a given society. They shape social relationships, regulate economic activities, and influence political processes. Consequently, understanding the operation of informal institutions is crucial for comprehending the complex dynamics of governance, power, and social order.

Moreover, the recognition and analysis of informal institutions provide valuable insights into the interplay between formal and informal sources of power and authority. By examining these unwritten rules and social practices, scholars can gain a deeper understanding of the intricate relationship between formal institutions and the social fabric of a society. This perspective illuminates the complex nature of social and political order, demonstrating how formal and informal institutions interact and shape the trajectory of governance and social dynamics.

Informal rules, unlike their formal counterparts, are not codified but are instead practised, deriving their relevance from their actual impact on societal behaviour. Informal institutions often compete with the state's authority to make binding decisions by establishing parallel areas of competence or, more commonly, by influencing the decision-making processes of the state itself (Lauth, 2000, 25). It is important to note that formal and informal institutions are interdependent and not mutually exclusive (Cheng and Womack, 1996).

In the context of democracies, formal and informal institutions can have various relationships with each other. Three types of relationships can be distinguished: Complementary, substitutive, and conflicting. In the complementary type, formal and informal institutions coexist side-by-side, reinforcing and supporting one another. The substitutive type occurs when either formal or informal institutions are functionally equivalent and effective in achieving the same outcomes. Finally, the conflicting type arises when the two systems of rules are incompatible and unable to harmonize (Lauth, 2000, 25).

Informal institutions, often referred to as the unwritten rules of political life, serve several functions. They fill gaps in formal institutions, coordinate the operation of overlapping and potentially conflicting institutions, and operate parallel to formal institutions in regulating political behaviour. These roles of informal institutions are associated with distinct patterns of institutional stability and change. Scholars have identified four types of informal institutions: complementary, accommodating, competing, and substitutive (Helmke and Levitsky, 2004, 727). The typology of informal institutions includes the following categories:

1. Complementary informal institutions: These institutions address issues that are not adequately covered by formal rules or help individuals achieve their goals within the formal institutional framework. They work in harmony with formal institutions and contribute to a more comprehensive governance system.
2. Accommodating informal institutions: In this category, formal rules are effective, but the outcomes diverge due to the influence of informal practices. Accommodating institutions provide flexibility within the formal system, allowing for diverse interpretations and implementation.
3. Competing informal institutions: When formal rules are ineffective, competing informal institutions emerge, leading to divergent outcomes. In this scenario, multiple sets of informal rules coexist and vie for authority, creating challenges and potential conflicts.
4. Substitutive informal institutions: In situations where formal institutions are ineffective, substitutive informal institutions take over and deliver convergent outcomes. These informal practices and arrangements effectively replace the formal system, fulfilling the roles and functions that formal institutions fail to address.

Recent scholarship has focussed on the dynamic interaction between informal and formal institutions, exploring how they complement, substitute for, accommodate, or undermine each other (Helmke and Levitsky, 2004). It is important to note that the relationship between formal and informal institutions is not fixed (Yilmaz, 2022a, 2022b).

Informal rules play a significant role in shaping the outcomes of formal institutions across various areas, including legislative politics, judicial politics, party organization, campaign finance, regime change, federalism, public administration, and state building (Helmke and Levitsky, 2004, 726). In many cases, informal institutions depend on the existence of formal institutions. They exist at the expense of formal institutions, exploiting them for their own purposes and either partially occupying or penetrating them. This parasitic nature is often expressed through phenomena such as corruption (Lauth, 2000, 26).

Existing typologies primarily focus on the interaction between informal institutions and an established framework of formal rules that are taken for granted. However, in transitional settings where formal institutions are in a state of flux, these typologies may be less applicable. Informal institutions have been categorized as specific types of relationships (e.g., clientelism, autocratic cliques, clientelist parties, mafia), forms of material exchange (corruption), exertion of violent influence (putsch threat, guerrilla warfare, riots, organized crime), civil resistance (civil disobedience), and legal practices (custom law) (Lauth, 2000, 27–43).

The relationship between formal and informal realms is complex, dynamic, and contextual. This relationship can be negative, positive, or double-edged, and informal institutions can contribute to the stabilization, change, collapse, or neglect of formal institutions (Lauth, 2000, 25–26; Levitsky and Helmke, 2006, 16–18). Informal institutions can replace, undermine, or reinforce formal institutions, regardless of the strength of the formal institutions themselves. Additionally, the competition among elites, driven by informal rules, further influences the dominant interactions that shape the development of the institutional framework (Grzymala-Busse, 2010, 311).

Formal institutions often obscure the significant impact of informal rules and norms, which are the actual rules that shape behaviour in many political regimes. The repertoire of informal institutions encompasses various forms, including special relationships such as autocratic cliques and mafia, violent exertion of influence through tactics like putsch threats, organized crime, extrajudicial executions, and material exchange practices such as corruption. Autocratic cliques operate within the state, while the mafia influences society at large. Autocratic cliques are characterized by limited access, hierarchical ties, and the ability to gather political support and exert direct influence (Lauth, 2000).

Some informal institutions are self-reinforcing, while others are externally enforced, sometimes even by the state itself. Informal institutions are defined as socially shared rules that are typically unwritten and enforced outside of officially sanctioned channels, whereas formal institutions consist of rules and procedures that are widely accepted as official (Helmke and Levitsky, 2006; Soyler, 2019).

Accommodating informal institutions are often created by actors who are dissatisfied with the outcomes produced by formal rules but are unable to change or openly violate those rules (Helmke and Levitsky, 2004). In contrast to traditional authoritarian regimes, electoral authoritarianism claims to embrace democracy while eschewing overt repression. Informal institutions serve as powerful tools for manipulation (Soyler, 2019).

The key distinction between autocracy and democracy lies not solely in the basic regime structure but rather in the function and validity of formal democratic institutions, which encompass rules and norms. In the grey zone between authoritarian regimes and consolidated democracies, formal institutions often mask specific informal institutions that, in reality, dictate behaviour and decision-making processes (O'Donnell, 1996; Lauth, 2000).

Customary law represents an additional informal institution that, by itself, holds a certain degree of influence, yet it realizes its complete impact upon validation by state entities. While its effect might seem borderline informal due to its reliance on state endorsement, it falls within the category of informal institutions due to its other defining characteristics (Lauth, 2000). The power of custom law to wield influence, as well as its distinguishing characteristic, is evident in the fact that it serves as a legal source for formal law, enabling the conversion of informal rules into formal ones (Lauth, 2000).

Custom law, in its various forms, exerts its influence on the political system in two significant ways. First, it engenders competition among different legal contents, which can manifest as complementarity, substitution, or undermining of the rule of law. Complementary forms of interaction work in favour of democracy, while the other two forms are evaluated as detrimental or even lethal to democracy. It is important to note that productive tensions, observed in cases of civil disobedience, are not present in this context (Lauth, 2000).

Secondly, custom law serves as a source for the creation of formal law. In this capacity, custom law can also be understood as a form of political participation, where rules are transferred into the political system, transcending specific material concerns. The effects of custom law on democracy vary depending on its particular character in each case, and its impact can be evaluated as either beneficial or harmful to democracy (Lauth, 2000).

The relationship between custom law and formal institutions is complex. While custom law displays elements of state sanction, it is considered an informal institution due to its distinct features and ability to shape formal legal frameworks. Its influence is not limited to its individual existence but extends to the confirmation and recognition it receives from state agencies. This recognition elevates custom law from a mere informal practice to a legal source that informs the creation of formal laws.

Moreover, custom law's impact on the political system is multifaceted. The competition between different legal contents reflects the dynamic nature of the interaction between custom law and formal institutions. The complementary forms of interaction, which support democracy, demonstrate the potential for informal institutions to enhance and complement formal legal structures.

Conversely, the substitutive and undermining forms of interaction pose challenges to the rule of law and can hinder democratic processes.

Furthermore, custom law's role in the creation of formal law highlights its significance as a mechanism for political participation. By transferring rules from the informal realm into the political system, custom law can shape the development of formal legal frameworks. The effects of this process can vary, depending on the specific characteristics and context of custom law. While some instances of custom law may contribute to strengthening democratic principles, others may have adverse effects, potentially undermining democratic values.

In summary, custom law occupies a unique position as an informal institution that interacts with formal institutions in complex ways. Its ability to influence and transform informal rules into formal ones distinguishes it as a significant factor in shaping legal frameworks. The competition between different legal contents and custom law's role in the creation of formal law illustrates its diverse effects on the political system. Understanding the dynamics and implications of custom law within the broader context of formal and informal institutions is crucial for comprehending the complexities of legal and democratic processes.

2.3 Legal Pluralism, Formal and Informal Law

A critical inquiry revolves around the essence of law: Does the state solely sanction a singular legal framework? The response is contingent on the definition of law itself and the theoretical perspectives adopted by researchers in elucidating socio-legal occurrences. Evidently, a universally accepted definition of law remains elusive, given the divergent approaches that accentuate either justice and morality or rules and regulations (Menski, 2000).

Traditionally, the study of law, often referred to as black-letter law, formalism, or legal positivism, has focussed on evaluating legal rules and cases as the primary subject matter (Fitzpatrick, 1983). Within the context of legal modernity, the nation-state has emerged as the central reference point for law, replacing mankind or religion. According to this understanding, the state is considered the sole source of law, and law is conceptualized as a distinct, uniform, coherent, autonomous, exclusive, and systematic hierarchical ordering of normative propositions (Galanter, 1966, 153–154). The power of the nation-state is asserted through law, which represents the codified, differentiated, institutionalized, and legitimized expression of state sovereignty and monopoly of power. Within this framework, law is seen as the command of the sovereign, and any rival normative orders are not recognized as law (Griffiths, 1986, 8). This state-centric view of law has been widely accepted by legal scholars, economists, and social and political scientists throughout the twentieth century, as they believed that law would lose its distinctive meaning if alternative normative orders were included (Von Benda-Beckmann and Turner, 2018, 262).

However, this state-centric approach has faced criticism for being parochial and limited in its scope. Scholars argue that it privileges the state (legocentrism) and territoriality (nationalist concerns) while neglecting the broader global context of law and its diverse manifestations (Menski, 2007, 198). Law extends beyond the boundaries of the state, encompassing religious laws, transnational laws, and international law. From a sociological perspective, law is not confined to formal legal acts, rules, administrative orders, or court decisions. It encompasses a wider range of normative systems and practices that influence social behaviour and shape governance (Soyler, 2019).

To develop a comprehensive understanding of law, it is necessary to recognize its pluralities and acknowledge the existence of multiple normative orders. This broader perspective allows for the exploration of legal phenomena beyond the confines of state-sanctioned law. It opens avenues to examine the interactions between different legal systems, such as customary law, religious law, and transnational legal frameworks. By adopting a more inclusive approach, researchers can develop globally acceptable methods of understanding law and its multifaceted nature, accounting for its various expressions, commonalities, and complexities (Von Benda-Beckmann and Turner, 2018). This shift in perspective encourages a deeper examination of the sociological dimensions of law and its relationship with broader social, cultural, and political contexts.

Socio-legal scholars and anthropologists have long recognized that law is not confined to a singular, monolithic entity sanctioned solely by the state. Instead, they have explored law as cognitive and normative orders that emerge and persist within various social fields, encompassing diverse communities, associations, and even transnational contexts. This broader understanding of law challenges the traditional view that emphasizes formal legal systems enacted by the nation-state as the exclusive source of law (Woodman and Allott, 1985).

Within these social fields, a multitude of normative orderings coexist alongside formal state law. These alternative legal orders include local customs, unofficially transplanted ethnic minority laws, religious laws, and other norm systems. Such legal pluralism, as it is often referred to, recognizes that state law is just one among many legal orders operating in society. It acknowledges that legal systems are not confined to a single, uniform framework but rather exhibit diverse expressions and coexist with varying degrees of legitimacy and authority (Griffiths, 1986).

Legal pluralism can be seen as the empirical reality that emerges when different modes of normative ordering are observed and practiced by individuals within a given society, regardless of state recognition. It encompasses a range of perspectives on law, from recognizing multiple legal orders within a nation-state to considering law as a more expansive concept that does not depend on state endorsement for its validity (Sack, 1986). This inclusive understanding of law acknowledges the existence of different normative systems, their diverse sources, and the complex dynamics of their interaction within a socio-legal context (Griffiths, 2002; Von Benda-Beckmann and Turner, 2018; Yilmaz, 2002, 2016a).

By recognizing the existence of legal pluralism, scholars seek to move beyond the narrow view of law as solely determined by state legislation and formal legal institutions. They explore the multifaceted nature of law, considering its intersection with cultural, social, and religious dimensions. In this broader perspective, law is understood as an evolving and dynamic phenomenon shaped by interactions between various normative orders and the practices of individuals and communities (Woodman and Allott, 1985).

The concept of legal pluralism underscores the complexity and richness of legal systems, emphasizing the need to go beyond a state-centric approach to law. It invites scholars to examine the coexistence, interaction, and potential tensions among different legal orders, shedding light on how individuals navigate and negotiate diverse normative landscapes. This expanded understanding of law enables a deeper analysis of the power dynamics, social hierarchies, and cultural complexities that shape legal phenomena within societies globally (Griffiths, 1986; Von Benda-Beckmann and Turner, 2018).

Moreover, legal pluralism challenges the assumption that law is a fixed and static entity. It recognizes the dynamic nature of normative orders, highlighting their potential for adaptation, negotiation, and change. In this sense, legal pluralism offers a more nuanced and inclusive framework for studying law, enabling researchers to explore the diverse sources of normativity and how legal systems and practices respond to social, cultural, and political transformations (Griffiths, 2002).

Griffiths (1986) distinguishes between two types of legal pluralism: Weak and strong. Weak legal pluralism occurs when the sovereign mandates different bodies of law for different groups within the population based on factors such as ethnicity, religion, nationality, or geography (Griffiths, 1986). These different legal systems are applied to specific segments of society and can take the form of native law, religious law, customary law, and personal law (Moore, 1978). In weak legal pluralism, the goal is often to achieve legal uniformity eventually. However, until that is accomplished, the sovereign allows and commands different bodies of law for different groups or communities.

Presently, countries like Pakistan and India exemplify weak legal pluralist systems, where religious minorities are granted the freedom to follow their own religious laws concerning personal matters such as marriage and inheritance.

On the other hand, strong legal pluralism refers to a socio-legal reality that exists without recognition or even in opposition to the state (Griffiths, 1986; Yilmaz, 2000, 2001). In societies deeply entrenched in a particular culture, it becomes exceedingly challenging to engineer and reshape the society according to desired norms. Although the constitutions of many developing countries may uphold a highly monistic legal framework on paper, in practice, a significant number of individuals resolve their personal and legal matters outside the purview of the official legal system. This signifies the existence of legal pluralism within these countries despite its disregard by the mainstream legal system of the nation-state (Tamanaha and Lehmann, 2021).

In strong legal pluralism, alternative normative systems and mechanisms of dispute resolution operate alongside or even in defiance of the state's legal framework. These informal legal systems may emerge from cultural traditions, community practices, or other forms of social organization. They often address a wide range of issues, including family matters, commercial disputes, and interpersonal conflicts, providing individuals and communities with alternative avenues for seeking justice and resolving conflicts (Tamanaha and Lehmann, 2021).

The existence of strong legal pluralism challenges the traditional view that the state is the sole source of law and the ultimate authority in resolving legal disputes. It highlights the importance of acknowledging and engaging with the diverse legal orders that operate within a society, even if they exist outside the formal legal system. The recognition of strong legal pluralism prompts scholars, policymakers, and legal practitioners to consider alternative approaches to legal regulation and dispute resolution, considering the lived experiences and preferences of the individuals and communities involved (Tamanaha and Lehmann, 2021).

Legal pluralism, as understood in anthropology, serves as a conceptual framework that recognizes situations in which individuals and communities draw upon multiple legal systems, regardless of their recognition within the state legal system (Von Benda-Beckmann and Turner, 2018). Alongside legal pluralism, there are alternative concepts that shed light on specific aspects of this phenomenon, including polycentrism, legalities, inter-legality, parallel legal orders, nomosphere, hybridity, vernacularization, iterations, lawfare, legal diversity, and more, each highlighting different facets of legal pluralism (Von Benda-Beckmann and Turner, 2018).

This anthropological perspective acknowledges that people, in their social and economic interactions, often rely on customary and religious laws or develop new unnamed legal systems, sometimes incorporating elements of state law, even in cases where the state explicitly denies the validity of these alternative legal forms (Von Benda-Beckmann and Turner, 2018). The notion of strong, deep, or new legal pluralism recognizes that legal pluralism is inherent in all societies, implying that multiple forms of social ordering exist and hold authority for members of a society, irrespective of state recognition (Griffiths, 2002).

It is important to note that Griffiths' seminal article on legal pluralism should not be interpreted as a value judgment opposing the state. Rather, Griffiths sought to demonstrate that a state-centric view of law overshadowed the significance of other legal systems at play in social interactions without making a positive or negative assessment of their content (Von Benda-Beckmann and Turner, 2018). Empirical studies on plural legal circumstances do not inherently evaluate the respective legal regimes as good or bad but rather aim to understand the complex dynamics and interactions within these pluralistic contexts (Zips and Weilenmann, 2011).

Anthropologists and legal scholars studying legal pluralism aim to provide a nuanced understanding of law as a multifaceted and socially embedded phenomenon. They emphasize the importance of recognizing and engaging with the diverse legal orders that coexist within a society, acknowledging the agency and autonomy of individuals and communities in shaping their own normative frameworks and dispute-resolution mechanisms. By embracing a broader perspective on law that goes beyond the boundaries of the state legal system, scholars can gain deeper insights into the complex realities of legal practice and how individuals navigate and negotiate multiple legal systems in their everyday lives.

Strong legal pluralism manifests itself in various ways and can have both positive and negative effects on the individuals and communities involved. Lazarev (2019) highlights the case of women in Chechnya who have benefited from the presence of a secular legal system, which has provided them with an alternative to the Sharia-based legal pluralistic system in the country. In this context, the objectivity and positivism of the modernist legal system have allowed women to escape the constraints imposed by cultural and religious gender roles, thereby benefiting them in traditional societies (Yilmaz, 2003).

Conversely, a history of forcefully imposing a uniformist approach to law has resulted in systemic institutional discrimination against indigenous cultures. Otis (2018) examines the case of Canada, where legal pluralism has been utilized as a means to promote human rights for indigenous populations. By allowing tribal communities to preserve their way of life and govern themselves according to their customs and beliefs, Canada acknowledges their right to self-determination and basic human freedoms.

The debate surrounding the merits and drawbacks of legal pluralism is not straightforward. It is shaped by highly complex contexts and specific cases. The effects of legal pluralism can vary depending on factors such as the legal systems involved, the social and cultural dynamics at play, and the power dynamics within the society. Therefore, it is crucial to approach the discussion on legal pluralism with an understanding of the nuanced and multifaceted nature of its impacts.

This book's central focus on the existence of informal Islamic laws, specifically Sharia, underscores the critical importance of strong legal pluralism. Sharia, the divine law rooted in the teachings of the Quran and Sunna, does not adhere to a simplistic set of rules but instead encompasses a vast body of texts comprising religious scriptures, hadith (prophetic traditions), and legal writings. These texts serve as the authoritative basis for Islamic legal thought and practice, making Sharia more than just the law contained within Muslim legal books. It extends to encompass the practical application of Islamic principles in the everyday lives of Muslims. The nature of Sharia as a diffuse legal system is marked by its lack of coherent codes and enforcement mechanisms, along with its reliance on multiple authorities and diverse sources of law (Gerber, 1994; Yilmaz, 2020).

For many Muslims, irrespective of its informal nature, Sharia assumes the role of a comprehensive order that governs all aspects of life, extending even to matters of protocol and etiquette (Hoffman, 1993). According to classical Islamic theory, law is perceived as the revealed will of God, existing independently of and predating the establishment of Muslim states. Rather than being subservient to Muslim society, Sharia exercises control over it (Yilmaz, 2003, 2016a, 2020). Islam, for many believers, is viewed as a comprehensive system encompassing the realms of state, society, law, thought, and art. Religion is seen as the unifying and prevailing factor in this civilization (Yilmaz, 2003). It is crucial to note that Islamic law, in its broadest sense, governs various spheres of life, with family law, in particular, being deeply intertwined with religious principles. As a result, Islamic law guides the legal consciousness, mental maps, and cognitive frameworks of Muslims, exerting significant influence over their lives. The allegiance demanded by Islam once an individual freely embraces it is perceived as an unbreakable bond uniting Muslims worldwide. Consequently, if conflicts arise between the laws of Muslim societies and secular legislation, Muslim mentality dictates that divine law, Sharia, should prevail (Yilmaz, 2003).

This principle of prioritizing divine law is not only relevant to Muslims residing in the West but also extends to their interactions within their respective nation-states. Muslims strive to contest, defend, and protect themselves against the authority of rational and secular systems, upholding the supremacy of Sharia (King, 1995). Therefore, it is not uncommon for many Muslims, both in Muslim-majority (Yilmaz, 2016b, 2022a; 2022b) and non-Muslim countries (Yilmaz, 2000, 2002), to seek alignment with Sharia rather than the specific legal frameworks of their nations, particularly concerning matters such as marriage, divorce, inheritance, and property (Nielsen, 1987; Speelman, 1995).

In sum, the coexistence of informal Islamic laws, derived from Sharia, alongside formal legal systems often leads to intricate interactions. This coexistence often creates a multifaceted dynamic where these systems interact and sometimes merge, leading to what is referred to as legal hybridity. The idea of recognizing the porous nature of legality highlights the fluidity and interplay among various legal frameworks. In this context, inter-legality emerges within the broader framework of strong legal pluralism. Inter-legality embodies the concept that different legal spaces, each with its own rules and norms, intersect and blend, influencing each other within a given societal context. This perspective acknowledges that legal systems are not always discrete and separate entities but rather interact and influence each other, shaping the legal landscape in intricate and sometimes unexpected ways. It's an acknowledgment of the dynamic nature of law, where formal and informal systems coexist, sometimes overlapping or converging, impacting societal norms and practices.

2.4 Sharia as Informal Law in the Lives of Western Muslims

The evolving situation of Muslims residing in non-Muslim societies necessitated new ijtihad in addressing their religious duties and life in Western environments. With Muslims relocating to Western lands, the need for guidance on religious obligations and navigating secular legal systems became pressing. To address these challenges, Islamic jurists formulated the minority fiqh (Fiqh Al-Aqalliyyat), a legal doctrine tailored to the needs of Muslims living as minorities in the West (Yilmaz, 2016b). In Western societies where Muslims constitute a minority, the interaction between Sharia or Islamic teachings and secular state laws introduces complexities. These complexities are particularly pertinent for the new generation of Muslims, navigating between the principles of Sharia and the legal frameworks of the secular state. Transitioning to Western contexts, discussions regarding minority fiqh in liberal democracies often raise debates regarding integration, adaptation, and the accommodation of Islamic principles within secular legal frameworks. Understanding the demographic composition and historical backgrounds of Muslim populations in Western countries becomes pivotal in comprehending the diversity and varying approaches within Sharia debates and practices.

The comprehensive exploration of Sharia, Islamic jurisprudence, and their interactions within diverse societal contexts illuminates the intricacies and nuances of these systems (Abdalla, 2012; Moazam, 2011; Abu-Odeh, 2004; Berger, 2006; Whyte, 2018). Pioneering the reformist approach, Azhari scholars Yusuf al-Qardawi and Taha Jabir al-Alwani began issuing fatwas in the 1990s, addressing the challenges faced by Muslims living in the West. Fiqh Al-Aqalliyyat emerged as a response, seeking to resolve conflicts between Islamic principles and Western values within the framework of Islamic jurisprudence. This legal doctrine aims to reinterpret Islamic concepts to accommodate life in non-Muslim countries, focussing on financial and political matters.

Issues like the validation of interest-based mortgages and participation in secular politics sparked extensive debates among Islamic scholars, with differing interpretations and oppositions. Scholars of Fiqh Al-Aqalliyyat strive to create a space for Muslims to navigate life without conflict between Sharia and Western lifestyles.

Living in the West, Islamic scholars have advocated for reforms in Islamic laws. Concepts like maqasid al-Shariah, combining reformist ideas with American Muslim exceptionalism, have emerged, aiming to reform Muslim societies and assert the uniqueness of American Muslims within the Western context. These reformist ideas have been shaped not only by the Western environment but also within Western societies, where certain Muslim communities and scholars view themselves distinctively within the broader Western Muslim community.

In the Western context, discussions surrounding different forms of fiqh often revolve around minority contexts. This particular aspect of Islamic legal practice in Western liberal democracies sparks considerable debate.

Critics of minority fiqh often characterize it as overly integrationist and apologetic, while proponents argue that it enables Muslims to apply Quranic teachings to new and unfamiliar settings (Whyte, 2018). However, before delving into the specifics of Islamic legal practice in the West, it is crucial to develop a deeper understanding of the demographic and historical composition of the Muslim population in these countries. This contextualization helps shed light on how different Muslim groups – ethnic, cultural, and religious – approach Sharia debates within their respective countries. Equally significant is understanding why some Western countries are more accepting of Sharia-compliant practices than others. By examining internal and external perspectives on Sharia debates and practices, this book aims to unpack the evolving legal landscape and the future of Muslim civil practices in Western democracies.

In the Western context, where Muslims constitute a minority, the understanding and expression of Sharia also vary. Unlike Muslim-majority countries, Muslims in the West live under constitutional laws that are either secular or derived from non-Muslim sources. In this context, understanding how the new generation of Muslims expresses their use of Sharia, and more fundamentally, their engagement with the concept itself, becomes a central research question for this book. How young Muslims navigate their lives between Sharia or Islamic teachings and the secular state emerges as a primary focus of inquiry. By exploring this dynamic, the book sheds light on the multifaceted relationship between Muslims, Sharia, and the broader legal framework within Western societies.

Sharia law, in the form of informal laws in Western countries, represents an order that governs all aspects of life, even extending to rules of protocol and etiquette (Hoffman, 1993). In the context of Western Muslims, the use of Sharia-driven or Islamic-driven practices in matters such as inheritance, marriage, dietary choices, celebration of events, and banking preferences exemplify informal laws. These laws exist outside the formal legal framework and are more influenced by religious beliefs. Within this realm of informal law, there is also room for plurality due to the theological differences among various subsects of Islam. Ghobadzdeh and Akbarzadeh (2015) highlight the significant polarization within larger sects of Sunnis and Shias on matters related to faith, which also extends to politics. For example, the practice of "nikah al-muta," or temporary marriage, is highly debated within Islam, and different sectarian groups and their sub-groups hold diverse views on the matter (Mahmood and Nye, 2013).

In the UK, which has the largest population of Muslims among the three case studies, there has been a significant debate surrounding the use of Sharia law, particularly in the context of family law and arbitration. Brechin (2013) highlights that while there is a need to make laws more responsive to the needs of the local community, Sharia-driven laws may sometimes conflict with human rights charters followed in the UK. Griffiths (2014) points out the problems associated with using Sharia or Jewish laws for the arbitration of "domestic issues," such as cases of domestic violence, as it can perpetuate ongoing abuse and leave perpetrators unpunished. Moreover, the lack of recognition of informal laws, such as polygamy practiced by Muslim men, places women and children from multiple marriages in legally precarious positions regarding divorce, alimony, child support, and inheritance (Serck, 2014). Despite these concerns, the Muslim Arbitration Tribunal has been operating within the civil jurisdiction in the UK since 2007 to assist Muslims. However, Zee (2014) argues that allowing these institutions to operate independently can lead to abuses and human rights violations, suggesting that the government should accommodate Sharia-driven informal entities to ensure compliance with international and domestic human rights standards.

In the USA, there are no formal tribunals that support or facilitate Sharia-driven legal pluralism. Muslims in the country often resort to private consultations with religious figures or practice Sharia in a personal capacity (Islamic Networks Group, n.d.). However, due to Islamophobia, various politicians in the US have called for a ban on Sharia, viewing it as a threat to the US Constitution and values (Fallon, 2013; Khan, 2012). Similarly, in Australia, the wave of Islamophobia has resulted in extreme reactions towards Sharia, such as the display by Pauline Hanson during her "burka" appearance in the Senate in 2017 (Murphy, 2017). In both the US and Australia, Sharia-driven informal laws also operate in the shadows.

Overall, it is evident that informal laws driven by Sharia exist within Muslim communities. This book aims to explore how young Muslims perceive this concept, whether they seek its formalization, desire a plural legal system, or are content with the existing formal laws. Additionally, the study investigates the sources of Sharia driven informal laws in the lives of young people and how this framework may or may not shape their civic activities and aspirations.

2.5 Conclusion

This chapter discussed the presence and influence of informal laws among Western Muslims that are driven by Sharia, the Islamic legal framework. These informal laws govern a wide range of aspects of their lives, including inheritance, marriage, dietary choices, celebrations, and banking practices. They exist outside the formal legal framework and are deeply influenced by religious beliefs and practices. One crucial aspect that emerged from our exploration is the presence of plurality within Islam. Theological differences among various subsects of the religion contribute to significant polarization, extending to matters of faith and politics.

By their very nature, informal laws serve as competitors to state-supported formal laws. The clash between these two systems is rooted in the informality of the former and the uniformity of the latter. State laws often lack the flexibility to accommodate parallel opinions on personal and collective matters of interest. As a response, informal laws emerge to address the diverse needs of various groups that may not be adequately met by formal laws.

Sharia law, when manifested as informal laws in Western countries, extends its influence beyond specific legal issues to encompass various aspects of life, including matters of protocol and etiquette. It shapes social norms and practices within Muslim communities. Throughout our exploration, we have encountered ongoing debates and challenges surrounding the acceptance and integration of Sharia-driven informal laws within the legal systems and societies of Western countries. In the United Kingdom, concerns have been raised about potential conflicts with human rights charters and their impact on women's rights in cases such as polygamy. In the United States and Australia, there is less formal recognition of Sharia-driven informal laws, but political rhetoric and Islamophobia have fuelled debates and calls for bans on Sharia.

In conclusion, this chapter has provided a comprehensive understanding of the presence and significance of Sharia-driven informal laws among Western Muslims. It has shed light on the complexities, debates, and challenges surrounding their acceptance, integration, and coexistence within legal systems and societies. By exploring the diverse perspectives and dynamics related to informal laws, we have gained valuable insights into how young Muslims perceive and engage with these alternative legal frameworks. The chapter sets the stage for further exploration in subsequent chapters, delving deeper into the nuanced experiences and implications of Sharia-driven informal laws among Western Muslims.

References

Abdalla, Mohamad. 2012. "Sacred Law in a Secular Land: To What Extent Should Sharī 'a Law be Followed in Australia?" *Griffith Law Review*, 21(3): 657–679.

Abu-Odeh, Lama. 2004. "Modernizing Muslim Family Law: The Case of Egypt." *Vanderbilt Journal of Transnational Law*, 37: 1043–1146.

Berger M. 2006. "Sharia Law in Canada – Also Possible in the Netherlands?' " In *Crossing Borders: Essays in European and Private International Law, Nationality Law, and Islamic Law in Honour of Frans Van Der Velden*, edited by P van Der Grinten and T Heukels. Alphen aan den Rijn: Kluwer.

Brechin, J. 2013. "A Study of the Use of Sharia Law in Religious Arbitration in the United Kingdom and the Concerns that this Raises for Human Rights." *Ecclesiastical Law Journal*, 15(3): 293–315. https://doi.org/10.1017/S0956618X13000434

Cheng, Tun-jen and Brantly Womack. 1996. "General reflections on informal politics in East. Asia." *Asian Survey*, 36: 320–337.

Fallon, S. M. 2013. "Justice for All: American Muslims, Sharia Law, and Maintaining Comity within American Jurisprudence." *Boston College International and Comparative Law Review*, 36: 153.

Fitzpatrick, Peter. 1983. "Law, Plurality and Underdevelopment." In *Legality, Ideology and the State*, edited by David Sugarman. London: Academic Press, 159–182.

Galanter, Marc. 1966. "The Modernization of Law." In *Modernization*, edited by Myron Weiner. New York and London: Basic Books, 153–165.

Gerber, Haim. 1994. *State, Society, and Law in Islam: Ottoman Law in Comparative Perspective*. Albany: State University of New York Press.

Ghobadzdeh, N. and Akbarzadeh, S. 2015. "Sectarianism and the Prevalence of 'Othering' in Islamic Thought." *Third World Quarterly*, 36(4): 691–704. https://doi.org/10.1080/01436597.2015.1024433

Griffiths, Anne. 2002. "Legal Pluralism." In *An Introduction to Law and Social Theory*, edited by R Banakar and M Travers. Oxford: Hart Publishing, 289–310.

Griffiths, Cerian. 2014. "Sharia and Beth Din Courts in the UK: Is Legal Pluralism Nothing More than a Necessary Political Fiction? *Studia Iuridica Toruniensia*, 15: 39–52. ISSN 1689-5258.

Griffiths, John. 1986. "What is Legal Pluralism?" *The Journal of Legal Pluralism and Unofficial Law*, 18: 1–55.

Grzymala-Busse, Anna. 2010. "The Best Laid Plans: The Impact of Informal Rules on Formal Institutions in Transitional Regimes." *Studies in Comparative International Development*, 45: 311–333.

Helmke, Gretchen and Levitsky, Steven. 2004. "Informal Institutions and Comparative Politics: A Research Agenda." *Perspectives on Politics*, 2: 725–740.

Hoffman, Murad. 1993. *Islam: The Alternative*. Reading: Garnet Publishing.

Islamic Networks Group. n.d. *A Closer Look at Sharia in the United States*. Accessed 12 April 2023. https://ing.org/resources/for-all-groups/answers-to-frequently-asked-questions/a-closer-look-at-Sharia-in-the-united-states/

Khan, S. A. 2012. "Sharia Law, Islamophobia, and the US Constitution: New Tectonic Plates of the Culture Wars." *University of Maryland Law Journal of Race, Religion, Gender & Class*, 12: 123.

King, Michael. 1995. "Introduction." In *God's Law Versus State Law: The Construction of Islamic Identity in Western Europe*, edited by Michael King. London: Grey Seal.

Lauth, Hans-Joachim. 2000. "Informal Institutions and Democracy." *Democratization*, 7: 21–50.

Lazarev, Egor. 2019. "Laws in Conflict: Legacies of War, Gender, and Legal Pluralism in Chechnya." *World Politics*, 71(4): 667–709.

Levitsky, Steven, and Gretchen Helmke. 2006. *Informal Institutions and Democracy: Lessons from Latin America*. Baltimore: Johns Hopkins University Press.

Mahmood, S. and Nye, C. 2013. "I Do . . . for Now. UK Muslims Revive Temporary Marriages." *BBC*. 13 May. www.bbc.com/news/uk-22354201

Menski, Werner F. 2000. *Comparative Law in a Global Context, The Legal Systems of Asia and Africa*. London: Platinium.

Menski, W. F. 2007. *Comparative Law in a Global Context: The Legal Systems of Asia and Africa*. 2nd ed. Cambridge and New York: Cambridge University Press.

Moazam, Farhat. 2011. "Sharia Law and Organ Transplantation: Through the Lens of Muslim Jurists." *Asian Bioethics Review*, 3(4): 316–332.

Moore, Sally Falk. 1978. *Law as Process: An Anthropological Approach*. London: Routledge and Kegan Paul.

Murphy, K. 2017. "Pauline Hanson Wears Burqa in Australian Senate While Calling for Ban." *The Guardian*. 17 August. www.theguardian.com/australia-news/2017/aug/17/pauline-hanson-wears-burqa-in-australian-senate-while-calling-for-ban

Nielsen, Jørgen S. 1987. *Muslims in Western Europe*. Edinburgh: Edinburgh University Press.

O'Donnell, G. A. 1996. "Illusions About Consolidation." *Journal of Democracy*, 7(2): 34–51. https://doi.org/10.1353/jod.1996.0034

Otis, Z. 2018. "Individual Choice of Law for Indigenous People in Canada: Reconciling Legal Pluralism with Human Rights." *University of California Irvine Law Review*, 8: 207.

Sack, Peter. 1986. "Legal Pluralism: Introductory Comments." In *Legal Pluralism. Proceedings of the Canberra Law Workshop VII*, edited by Peter Sack and Elizabeth Minchin. Canberra: Research School of Social Sciences (Australian National University), 1–16.

Serck, L. 2014. "Polygamy in Islam: The Women Victims of Multiple Marriage." *BBC*. 1 June 2012. www.bbc.com/news/uk-england-berkshire-18252958

Soyler, Mehtap. 2019. "Conceptual Travel: Methodological Approaches", in Berrin Ceylan Ataman, Gülçin Taşkıran (editors) *Informal Institutions, and Democracy:*

Recent Evaluations on Humanities & Social Sciences. London: IJOPEC Publication Limited, 69–83.

Speelman, G. 1995. "Muslim Minorities and Shari ah in Europe." In *Religion, Law and Society: A Christian–Muslim Discussion*, edited by Tarek Mitri. Geneva, Kampen: WCC Publications/Kok Pharos.

Tamanaha, Z. Brian and Lehmann, S. Johan. 2021. *Legal Pluralism Explained: History, Theory, Consequences.* New York: Oxford University Press.

Von Benda-Beckmann, Keebet and Turner, Bertram. 2018. "Legal Pluralism, Social Theory, and the State." *The Journal of Legal Pluralism and Unofficial Law*, 50: 255–274.

Woodman, Gordon R. and Antony, Allott, eds. 1985. *People's Law and State Law. The Bellagio Papers.* Dordrecht: Foris Publications.

Whyte, Shaheen. 2018. "Whither Minority Jurisprudence: The Case of Fiqh Aqalliyat." *The Australian Journal of Islamic Studies*, 2(3): 55–75.

Yilmaz, Ihsan. 2000. "Muslim Law in Britain, Reflections in the Socio-Legal Sphere and Differential Legal Treatment." *Journal of Muslim Minority Affairs*, 20(2): 353–360. https://doi.org/10.1080/713680357

Yilmaz, Ihsan. 2001. "Law as Chameleon: The Question of Incorporation of Muslim Personal Law into the English Law." *Journal of Muslim Minority Affairs*, 21(2): 297–308.

Yilmaz, Ihsan. 2002. "The Challenge of Post-Modern Legality and Muslim Legal Pluralism in England." *Journal of Ethnic and Migration Studies*, 28(2): 343–354.

Yilmaz, Ihsan. 2003. "Non-Recognition of Post-Modern Turkish Socio-Legal Reality and Predicament of Women." *British Journal of Middle Eastern Studies*, 30(1): 25–41.

Yilmaz, Ihsan. 2016a. *Muslim Laws, Politics and Society in Modern Nation States: Dynamic Legal Pluralisms in England, Turkey and Pakistan.* London and New York: Routledge.

Yilmaz, Ihsan. 2016b. "Micro-Mujtahids and Implementation of Fiqh al-Aqalliyat." In *Rethinking Islamic Law for Minorities: Towards a Western-Muslim Identity*, edited by Jasser Auda. London: Association for Muslim Social Scientists.

Yilmaz, Ihsan. 2020. "Muslims, Sacred Texts, and Laws in the Modern World." In *Handbook of Contemporary Islam and Muslim Lives*, edited by M. Woodward and R. Lukens-Bull. Cham: Springer, 1–18.

Yilmaz, Ihsan. 2022a. *Authoritarianism, Informal Law, and Legal Hybridity: The Islamisation of the State in Turkey.* Singapore: Palgrave Macmillan.

Yilmaz, Ihsan. 2022b. "Use of Civilisational Populist Informal Law by Authoritarian Incumbents to Prolong Their Rule." *Religions*, 13(10): 960. https://doi.org/10.3390/rel13100960

Zee, Machteld. 2014. "Five Options for the Relationship between the State and Sharia Councils: Untangling the Debate on Sharia Councils and Women's Rights in the United Kingdom." *Journal of Religion and Society*, 16. https://ssrn.com/abstract=2380066

Zips, Werner and Markus, Weilenmann, eds. 2011. *The Governance of Legal Pluralism: Empirical Studies from Africa and Beyond.* Wien, Berlin: Lit. ISBN978-3-7000-0517-9. 304p.

3 Understanding Faith through Sharia

3.1 Introduction

This chapter aims to provide a detailed exploration of the various factors that influence their connection with faith, shedding light on their diverse experiences and perspectives. One significant factor discussed in this chapter is the role of family in shaping participants' religious identity. Many participants attribute their religious beliefs and practices to the influence of their parents or immediate family members. They describe how their upbringing and the teachings they received at home have played a crucial role in their understanding and practice of Islam. The chapter looks at the dynamics within families and examines how the transmission of religious knowledge and practices occurs through generations. It explores the intergenerational transmission of faith and how participants navigate their religious identity within the context of their family relationships.

The impact of the Muslim community on participants' faith is another important aspect explored in this chapter. Participants who actively engage with the community through mosque activities, religious events, and social gatherings express a stronger sense of connection to their faith. They find support, guidance, and a sense of belonging within the community, which reinforces their religious identity and commitment to Islam. The chapter aims to understand the experiences of participants within the Muslim community, highlighting the role of communal rituals, social interactions, and collective worship in shaping their religious beliefs and practices. It also examines the diverse range of Muslim communities and how the participants' experiences differ based on factors such as geographic location, cultural background, and the diversity within the Muslim community itself.

Personal experiences are another important aspect explored in the chapter. Participants reflect on how their own experiences, both positive and negative, have shaped their faith. These experiences could range from personal encounters with discrimination (Yilmaz 2000, 2001) and Islamophobia (Yilmaz 2016) and discrimination to positive interactions with individuals from diverse backgrounds that strengthened their religious beliefs. The chapter looks into how participants navigate and interpret their personal experiences within the

DOI: 10.4324/9781003482604-3

framework of their faith and how these experiences contribute to their understanding of Islam and its relevance in their lives.

Societal influences, such as media portrayals and public perceptions of Islam, are also discussed in relation to their impact on participants' connection with faith. Participants reflect on how these broader societal factors shape their relationship with Islam and influence their understanding and practice of the religion. The chapter examines the challenges participants face in reconciling their personal beliefs with external narratives and stereotypes about Islam. It also explores the strategies participants employ to navigate and respond to societal influences, including seeking knowledge, engaging in dialogue, and challenging misconceptions.

3.2 Significance of Faith and Its Diverse Meanings

The primary socialization of the participants was their first exposure to faith. Nadimah, who lived in Australia, explained how her environment was essential in creating awareness of Islam for her,

> Islam has been a very important thing for me for my life. It was the one thing that I opened my eyes to tha, from seeing your family praying together, to Ramadan, and to spending time with them and my family to Muharram as well, because we are part of the Shia faith.

Across the continent, in the UK, Rizwan also attributed his parents as the main reason for his connection with faith. He explained how faith became a relevant and instrumental part of his life,

> Yeah, my parents instilled religion in me when I was growing up and so it was pretty important, yeah.

In the United States, a similar sentiment was echoed. For example, Zia explained the significance of faith, which was attributed to childhood memories,

> Everything I do, my whole personality, is based around my faith. It had everything to do with the way I was raised. . . . If I wasn't the person I'm supposed to be as a Muslim, I wouldn't be who I am today. I would have reacted to situations differently. And I do fast and pray regularly.

The interviews conducted as part of this study shed light on the evolving nature of the relationship individuals have with faith as they transition from childhood to adulthood. It became apparent that beyond the early years of being taught religion by their parents, many participants embarked on a personal journey of exploring and seeking answers to fundamental questions about faith.

Some individuals, such as Jameelah, as they matured, developed a deeper understanding of Islam and recognized its significance in their lives. For someone like Jameelah, as she grew older, she understood the significance of religion. This indicates that many of the relationships with religion are dynamic. The young Australian Muslim narrated,

> It was part of my upbringing, and it changed – like you are never really the same, obviously, as you grow older you grow more wiser – it is definitely a big part of my life.

They actively engaged with their faith, delving into religious texts, seeking knowledge from scholars, and participating in religious activities. This process of personal exploration allowed them to form a more meaningful and informed connection with their religion. It highlights the dynamic nature of the relationship with faith, where individuals actively invest time and effort in deepening their understanding as they grow older.

However, it is important to note that not all participants followed the same trajectory. Some individuals experienced a distancing from their faith as they reached adulthood. Factors such as exposure to different worldviews, cultural influences, personal experiences, or questioning of religious doctrines contributed to this shift. These individuals may have chosen to explore alternative belief systems, adopt a more secular outlook, or detach themselves from religious practices altogether.

The dynamic nature of the relationship with faith underscores individual agency and autonomy in shaping one's religious beliefs and practices. It emphasizes that faith is not a static concept but an ongoing process of personal discovery and interpretation. The experiences shared by the participants in the interviews illustrate the diverse paths individuals may take in their journey with religion, ranging from a deeper engagement and connection to a more detached or distant stance.

Sohrab, who had Albanian ancestry, explained how his parents and grandparents were stripped of religiosity under Soviet Rule. He never really experienced a religious upbringing, even after his family moved to the United States. However, as he reached adulthood, he chose to explore his faith,

> I've never went to a mosque . . . The first time I went to a mosque. . . . I actually went inside a mosque for my dad's funeral, which was when I was 13. And I just, I didn't really even know what to do. Like, I saw people praying. I had no idea how to pray. I was never taught how to pray. One thing that kind of connected me to my religion was we had this plaque on the wall that had Quran's verses.

Melek shared how, in addition to the family, it was also the Muslim community – a school – that led to her exploring faith. She explained how moving to a school with Muslim students encouraged her to explore her faith,

> So, when once I moved to a school that was surrounded by so many Muslims, I learned so much about the religion, and that is, I think, I was

> more involved with my religion when I was independent, rather than from my family or my upbringing as a child.

Among the interviewees, a significant subset consisted of individuals who had converted to Islam. For these participants, the element of self-discovery and contemplation played a particularly crucial role in their journey towards embracing the faith. Unlike those who were born into Muslim families, their decision to convert involved a deliberate and conscious exploration of Islam as a religious and spiritual path.

The process of conversion to Islam often entailed a period of deep introspection, research, and soul-searching. These individuals embarked on a personal quest to seek truth and meaning, and in doing so, they evaluated their existing beliefs and ideologies. This involved engaging with Islamic teachings, studying the Quran, seeking guidance from knowledgeable individuals, and reflecting upon their own spiritual experiences.

The decision to convert to Islam represented a transformative turning point in their lives, marking a conscious choice to embrace the principles and practices of the faith. Their journey involved a profound personal transformation and a reorientation of their worldview and values. In this context, self-discovery and contemplation played a pivotal role as they explored and sought alignment between their inner beliefs and the teachings of Islam.

Through this process, converts often experienced a profound sense of connection and resonance with the principles and values espoused by Islam. They found solace, guidance, and a renewed sense of purpose in their newfound faith. The element of self-discovery and contemplation allowed them to delve deeply into their own spiritual yearnings and find a religious path that resonated with their personal beliefs and aspirations.

The experiences of converts highlight the significance of personal agency and conscious decision-making in matters of faith. Their choice to embrace Islam involved a profound personal commitment and a transformative process of self-exploration. By sharing their stories and insights, this study acknowledges the unique journey of converts and offers a glimpse into the transformative power of self-discovery and contemplation in the context of embracing Islam.

Moreover, the experiences of converts contribute to the broader understanding of the diversity within the Muslim community. Their unique perspectives and backgrounds enrich the beliefs and practices within the religion, underscoring the importance of inclusivity and acceptance of individuals from various religious backgrounds and paths. As their parents were not Muslims, it was their decision as teenagers or young adults to convert to Islam. One such story was shared by Habiba, who lives in the US,

> I was raised a Catholic, and I became a Muslim when I was 17. Sixteen years old, actually. My family was somewhat religious. I think there were some times in my life when we went to church more than others.

> I consider myself quite religious. I try to pray five times a day. Don't always do it. But religion is a really important part of my life. And I do it fast.

As young Muslims grew older, they experienced a range of perspectives and choices regarding their level of religiosity and attachment to faith. This stage of life presented them with the opportunity to reflect on their beliefs, values, and personal convictions and make decisions about the role of religion in their lives.

For some individuals, the journey of maturing and gaining independence led them to develop a stronger connection to their faith. They found themselves drawn closer to Islam as they sought solace, guidance, and a sense of purpose in its teachings. This could be a result of personal experiences, spiritual growth, or a deepening understanding and appreciation of the moral and ethical principles of Islam. These individuals actively engaged with religious practices, such as prayer, fasting, and participation in community events, as they embraced their faith more fully.

On the other hand, there were young Muslims who expressed a desire to distance themselves from faith as they entered adulthood. This decision was often driven by personal introspection, critical questioning, or a shift in their worldview and priorities. They may have felt that certain aspects of religious practice or dogma did not resonate with their personal beliefs or values. This distancing from faith could also be influenced by social, cultural, or intellectual factors, as individuals sought to forge their own path separate from the religious traditions they were raised in.

Fatimah, who lives in Australia, explained this experience,

> So, religion was quite a big part of my life while I was growing up, like, I considered myself to be super religious, like, I used to wear a scarf, fasted, I prayed like four or five times a day. It is not a big part of my life now. I think since I turned 18, I have gotten to be quite liberal in my views, and I think Islam now is like what Christianity is to, like, everyday Australians, like, something I think about and celebrate but not something I actively participate in all the time kind of thing.

Zakaria also felt similarly as he discussed the dwindling role of faith in his life,

> It was definitely part of my life; it was very important growing up, and that importance has slowly diminished as I have grown older.

Omar, a young Australian, attributed this change to having the independence to think and choose for oneself,

> Well, growing up, you know, surrounded by a lot of people that are religious, and so obviously that rubbed off on me and, yeah, because

> as a child you were kind taught the values you know that you have to uphold as a Muslim and just the action that you need to take to uphold that. So, yeah, definitely when I was younger, we had more of an influence, but as I grow older and grew more independent, it has become less and less.

Imran shared his uncertainties about his view of religion in his life. In an honest discussion, he shared that he was not sure if he was "religious" but felt certain that his upbringing left him with a lot of knowledge about Islam. The young Australian explained,

> I am not religious . . . but I know my religion and beliefs and everything, so when it comes to the religious part – I don't know, I am not religious, but, like, I do have a lot of information about my religion. So, I don't know how you would rate that?

Hakeem felt that this choice for him meant that he was now a "cultural Muslim." He explained this term in the following way,

> Like I said, you know, religion has taught me a lot of values that I stand by, but in terms of how religious I am, I wouldn't say I am very religious, and like I said, I am not a practicing Muslim as well . . . So, I guess, you know, I was introduced to it by family, but how deep I have decided to go into the religion is probably up to me.

Imran, who lived in the US at the time of the interviews, explained how he became a cultural Muslim,

> To a good extent, but I describe myself as a cultural Muslim. Where quite a few years ago, I kind of stopped believing in the faith, but I have realized that – let us say that even if I were born a Christian, I would be in a similar position where I don't have to believe fully but I just kind of take part in it, as heritage in a way.

The freedom to make choices about their level of religiosity or attachment to faith is an important aspect of personal autonomy and self-determination. It reflects the diversity of individual experiences and perspectives within the Muslim community, acknowledging that each person's journey is unique and shaped by a variety of factors.

It is essential to recognize that the decision to distance oneself from faith does not necessarily equate to rejecting religious or spiritual values altogether. Rather, it signifies a personal choice to explore alternative paths, beliefs, or worldviews that align more closely with their individual identity and aspirations.

3.3 Expression of Faith

The expression of faith among young Muslims exhibited a wide range of manifestations, reflecting the multifaceted nature of religious belief and practice. Each individual's understanding and experience of faith were shaped by their unique circumstances, personal convictions, and cultural context.

For some participants, faith served as a guiding moral compass in their lives. It provided a set of ethical principles and values that influenced their decision-making and behaviour. These individuals found solace and guidance in their religious teachings, striving to align their actions with the teachings of Islam. Faith served as a moral anchor, helping them navigate challenges and dilemmas by seeking guidance from religious texts and the teachings of scholars.

For others, faith was a powerful identity marker. It represented an integral part of their personal and communal identity, shaping how they perceived themselves and how they were perceived by others. They embraced their Muslim identity with pride and found a sense of belonging within the Muslim community. Their faith was not merely a set of beliefs and practices but a core aspect of their overall identity that influenced their social interactions, lifestyle choices, and community involvement.

In some cases, the expression of faith took on performative aspects. This means that individuals emphasized outward rituals and practices associated with Islam, such as regular prayer, fasting, or wearing religious attire. These individuals viewed the performative aspects of faith as a means of demonstrating their devotion and adherence to religious obligations. They saw these practices as a form of worship and a means of connecting with the divine.

Interestingly, among the interviewees from Australia, there was a notable emphasis on the spiritual dimension of religion. For these individuals, faith went beyond the external rituals and cultural aspects of Islam. They sought a deeper spiritual connection with their Creator, engaging in practices such as meditation, contemplation, and the seeking of spiritual enlightenment. Their faith was centred on personal spirituality, inner reflection, and the pursuit of a closer relationship with God.

It is important to recognize that these expressions of faith are not mutually exclusive, and many individuals described a combination of these elements in their religious lives. The diverse expressions of faith among young Muslims highlight the individualized and multifaceted nature of religious experiences, where individuals navigate their own unique paths in understanding and expressing their faith.

Anas explained that the matter of faith was a spiritual one for him,

> I would say that, like, I guess, I am religious . . . I would say that I am a religious person, but I am more inclined to the spiritual and inner dimension you know of my religion. I don't really go too much towards, like, dogma or political aspects of religion or faith. It is more of a personal

> thing to me and like a spiritual kind of thing, but I would definitely say I am a religious person.

Noor, who also lived in Australia, focussed on the spiritual side of faith compared to ritualistic aspects, as she explained,

> Well, for me, religion gives me strength, so it is that sanctuary to me that I go to when I feel like the rest of life is collapsing. Islam has always benefited me in terms of, I feel like a much better person, my day-to-day life has become a lot easier, personally my own mental health and mental well-being and even physically, my habits have changed, and my temperament has changed towards good. So, it has never been more positive, and I am so ever grateful that I have found love in Islam.

Aisha, who is also Australian, elaborated on the spiritual and moral benefits of the practical aspects of faith. She discussed the five pillars of Islam,

> So, we have five fundamentals in religion that we observe, and so those, to me, are quite important, so you have fasting, prayer, charity, hajj, and shahadat – which means to acknowledge the oneness of God. For me, these five broken down teach me religion. So, fasting would represent patience, prayer would represent, you know, commitment and gratitude, and generosity in charity, so those tie in together. So, all of those can be broken down really beautifully, and I know outside of an Islamic faith, I couldn't have been exposed to those just as much as I am in this faith, but it did help in that I was practicing something so much, and I learnt that these are crucial and I have to be constantly thinking of others, for instance, in the case of Zakat, and be as patient as I can be with trying to have harmonious relationships with others or just outside of my life.

For a significant number of individuals, religion played a central role in shaping their identity and purpose in life. Their faith was not just a peripheral aspect of their existence but served as a guiding principle that permeated all aspects of their lives. These individuals viewed their religious beliefs as fundamental to their sense of self, their worldview, and their overall purpose in life.

For them, religion was not confined to specific times or places of worship; rather, it extended to every decision they made, big or small. Whether it was choices related to personal relationships, education, career, or even mundane daily activities, their faith served as a moral compass that directed their actions and guided their behaviour. They saw their religious beliefs as providing a clear framework for making ethical choices and leading a purposeful life.

These individuals often sought to align their decisions with the teachings and principles of their faith. They looked to religious scriptures, guidance from religious leaders, and personal reflection to inform their choices. Their commitment to their religious beliefs went beyond mere rituals and extended to a deep integration of faith into their thoughts, values, and actions.

This strong integration of religion into their identity influenced how they interacted with others and the world around them. They sought to embody the values of compassion, justice, and integrity that they derived from their faith, and they saw themselves as ambassadors of their religious tradition in their interactions with others.

Zubeida from Britain explained the role of faith as all-encompassing in her life,

> A 100%, it basically shapes my everyday life but also my wider purpose. Basically, it encompasses my whole life, I would say.

Khalifa from the US also shared a similar conviction,

> Yeah, pretty much everything I've been brought up has been guided by religion.

Taslimah, who lives in Australia, explained this theme with examples,

> You know how you make decisions on a daily basis? I would say I would make it revolve around my prayers, so, that is one thing that definitely tells me that religion is definitely the centre of me like the way . . . I think it is just easier that way, and I think I am not a really decisive person, so I always go to my religion. What would I do? Given I am a Muslim, or what I should do in Quran or hadith, like that. So, it is really like my call, you know, just your moral system in the background that is always running.

Zeeshan from the UK also felt similarly,

> For example, the decisions I make about where I'm going to eat today are shaped by my religion. If I have to go to a restaurant, I'll have to make a decision on where that restaurant is and what I'm going to eat there. Because as a Muslim, I have to make sure that the food is halal or things like that. So, that shapes my identity and I think that plays a big part.

Safdar, who lives in the US, explained how the ritual aspects of Islam are instrumental to him,

> Yes, I would say that religion is a strong, you know, strong structure in my life, and I believe that I do fast in Ramadan every year, I do pray regularly, and my religion is very important to me.

Lailah, an Australian who wears a hijab, explained how both spiritual and practical aspects mean that religion was part of her life,

> I wear a hijab; it is part of me every day, so I go out, and immediately I get described as a Muslim person. I pray, I fast, I go to the religious centre every week – well, not every week, but whenever there is something on. Yeah, it is part of who I am.

The experiences of these individuals highlight the transformative power of religion and its ability to provide a sense of identity, purpose, and moral guidance. By integrating their faith into their daily lives, they found meaning and a sense of direction that influenced their choices and interactions with the world.

It is important to note that this deep connection between faith and identity does not imply a lack of critical thinking or blind adherence to religious teachings. Many individuals who emphasized the importance of religion in their identity also engaged in thoughtful reflection, intellectual exploration, and theological discussions to deepen their understanding of their faith. Their commitment to their religion was rooted in a conscious choice and a personal conviction that shaped their worldview.

3.4 Faith and Identity

The interviews conducted as part of the three case studies revealed a common thread among young Muslims living in the West: The centrality of religion as a form of identification in their lives. While this identification is largely self-selected, based on their personal beliefs and values, it is also influenced by societal factors and sometimes imposed upon them along with their ethnic identity.

For many young Muslims, their religious identity serves as a significant aspect of their overall sense of self. It is not uncommon to find that they prioritize their religious affiliation as a key marker of their identity, alongside their national or ethnic background. They view their faith as an integral part of who they are and find solace, meaning, and belonging in their religious community.

In some cases, individuals actively choose to embrace their religious identity as a way of connecting with their heritage, cultural roots, and spiritual beliefs. They take pride in their Muslim identity and see it as a source of strength, resilience, and shared values. This self-selection of religious identification allows them to navigate the challenges and complexities of living in a multicultural and diverse society while maintaining a sense of belonging to their faith community.

Aqil, who is an Australian, explained how his name usually gives away his religion. This is something unintentional, but it has become part of his identity. The youth explained,

> I prefer, myself, to tell people that I am African, Muslim, Australian young African. I don't describe a lot of stuff about myself. As my name

> itself says, its . . . that is my full name, so basically, they already know that I am Muslim. So, like, I am proud of that, I am proud to be Muslim. So, yeah.

Among the women participants in the three countries, their choice of clothing emerged as a significant aspect that made Islam an inherent part of their identity. The decision to wear clothing that aligns with Islamic principles, such as hijab or modest attire, was seen as a visible expression of their faith and a marker of their Muslim identity.

For these women, the choice of clothing became a means of embodying their religious beliefs and values in their daily lives. By adhering to Islamic dress codes, they felt a sense of connection to their faith, a way to assert their Muslim identity, and a visible representation of their commitment to their religious practices.

The decision to wear Islamic clothing was not solely determined by external factors or societal expectations. Rather, it was often a personal and deeply meaningful choice rooted in their understanding of their faith and a desire to uphold its teachings. The clothing choice represented their agency and autonomy in expressing their religious beliefs and values.

It is important to note that the experiences and reasons behind the choice of clothing may vary among individual women. While some may see it as a form of empowerment and an expression of their religious convictions, others may have different motivations, such as cultural or family expectations, personal preference, or a desire to conform to social norms within their community.

By wearing Islamic clothing, these women also faced various social interactions and experiences, including encounters with stereotypes, biases, and sometimes even discrimination. Their choice of clothing not only made them more visible as Muslims but also made them susceptible to external perceptions and judgments based on preconceived notions about Islam and Muslim women.

Zulaikha, from the UK, explained her experience as a hijab wearer,

> Because for me, my religion is my defining factor. My hijab is a defining factor, and people see me as a Muslim woman.

Adeelah, who lives in Australia as a student, shared a similar experience,

> I guess with my hijab, I get people to know at first time, so I will straightly say that I am a Muslim student from Indonesia.

Similarly, Asifah, an Australian, discussed how this identification was a matter of pride for her,

> I do consider myself Muslim, of course, but I don't like saying it out loud because of the scarf; it should be enough of a statement like, "okay she

> is a Muslim, and she is also proud of it" because yeah. It is something that I do with pride.

Zohaib's perspective sheds light on how religion becomes central to the identity of Muslims living in non-Muslim majority countries. According to Zohaib, the experience of being a minority in a different cultural and religious context prompts Muslims to closely associate with their faith, making it a fundamental part of their identity.

Living as a religious minority often presents unique challenges and opportunities for individuals to navigate their religious and cultural identities. Zohaib likely expressed that being in a non-Muslim majority country can foster a stronger sense of connection to Islam, as it becomes a distinguishing factor and a source of solidarity within the Muslim community.

In such contexts, Muslims may seek solace, support, and a sense of belonging through their religious practices and beliefs. Religion can provide a framework for navigating cultural differences, establishing a sense of community, and preserving cultural traditions and values in a foreign environment.

Additionally, Zohaib's viewpoint suggests that the experience of being a minority can heighten the significance of religion as a means of preserving cultural heritage and resisting assimilation. For many Muslims, practicing their faith becomes a way to maintain their distinct cultural identity and counteract the potential erosion of their traditions and values in a different cultural context.

Furthermore, religion can serve as a source of resilience and empowerment for Muslims living in non-Muslim majority countries. It can provide them with a sense of purpose, guiding principles, and a moral compass to navigate the complexities of their daily lives. By embracing their faith, individuals like Zohaib may find strength and conviction in their religious beliefs, allowing them to overcome the challenges they face as minorities and contribute to their communities actively.

Zohaib's perspective highlights the transformative role of religion in shaping the identity of Muslims living outside of Muslim-majority countries. It emphasizes how the experience of being a minority in a different cultural and religious context can strengthen the significance and centrality of Islam in the lives of individuals, enabling them to find meaning, belonging, and resilience in their faith. He said,

> I mean, being raised in the West, you do really talk about religion, like people from coloured backgrounds are usually working-class backgrounds, so they are stuck in certain areas in London or whatever, like there are sometimes like their national British identity is not that strong and that would be because of the places they are. They also don't live in the country of their origin. Well, most people do have some sense of national identity, and I think most people do. I think Muslims in diaspora, the religion becomes more important, or it is an identity based

> around Islam, where it is negative or positive. Islam is something to be liked, like a central part of Muslim identity in the West.

Sana, also from the UK, discussed how religion becomes a defining feature of her identity. In her view, religion is a way of life which distinguishes her from others,

> The reason why I say British Muslim is because I understand that we have a religion that we adhere to. You know, growing up as a Muslim, you have certain stuff that you have to follow in Islam. So, I say British Muslim because you're associating yourself with that religion. You've got your own group, basically.

Rahima's experience provides another perspective on how faith can become the most pronounced part of identity for Muslims living in non-Muslim majority countries. In Rahima's case, her faith and religious practices, including wearing the hijab and following the tenets of Islam, take precedence over her ethnic identity. She explained this in the following manner,

> Like I would say to people, like, I am Muslim first rather than saying I am Pakistani. I also wear hijab, so usually, even before I say it is quite obvious. Secondly, you know, I am not really national like a nationalistic kind of person. Like, I do not really identify with a specific country, because I was born in Pakistan, but we moved to England when I was just one month old and then moved to Australia when I was 15 years old. So, I see myself as Pakistani British and Australian, so in terms of that, I just like to get it mixed up. So, like mainly Muslim is my main identity.

Rahima's emphasis on her faith rather than ethnicity indicates that her religious identity plays a significant role in shaping her sense of self and how she interacts with the world around her. The decision to wear the hijab, in particular, is a visible expression of her religious beliefs and serves as a clear marker of her Muslim identity.

By prioritizing her faith-based identity over her ethnic background, Rahima highlights the transformative power of religion in shaping one's self-perception and social interactions. For her, Islam provides a strong foundation for her values, principles, and sense of purpose. It influences her choices, behaviours, and worldview, allowing her to navigate the challenges and opportunities of living in a non-Muslim majority country with a sense of conviction and authenticity.

Rahima's experience also reflects the complexity of identity formation among Muslims in the diaspora. While ethnicity and cultural heritage undoubtedly play a role in shaping one's identity, Rahima's emphasis on her religious identity suggests that Islam has become the primary lens through which she views herself and engages with the world. This shift may stem from a desire to maintain a strong connection to her faith and to assert her religious beliefs in the face of societal norms and expectations.

Furthermore, Rahima's experience underscores the significance of personal agency in shaping one's identity. By actively choosing to embrace her religious identity, including wearing the hijab, Rahima exercises autonomy and control over how she presents herself to the world and how she defines her sense of self.

The high occurrence of the word "Muslim" and its variations demonstrates the strong association of the participants with their religious identity. It signifies their self-identification as Muslims and highlights the salience of Islam in their lives. Additionally, the recurrence of the word "religion" emphasizes its importance as a defining characteristic for these individuals.

The presence of terms like "proud" and "part" in relation to Muslim identity signifies a positive and integral connection between faith and self-perception. The participants express pride in their Muslim identity and view it as an integral part of who they are. This suggests a sense of ownership and active engagement with their religious beliefs and practices.

The diverse relationships participants have with faith further illustrate the multifaceted nature of religious identity. Some individuals inherit their religious beliefs and practices through their upbringing, indicating the intergenerational transmission of faith. For many participants, religion serves as a comprehensive ethical framework and a code of life, guiding their behaviours, decisions, and interactions with others. The spiritual dimension of religion is also evident, with some perceiving it as a source of personal connection, solace, and guidance. Furthermore, religion takes on a cultural dimension for a few participants, becoming a symbol of their heritage and cultural identity.

The variety of ways faith is understood and experienced highlights the unique and individual nature of religious identity among young Muslims in the West. It reflects the diverse backgrounds, perspectives, and journeys of these individuals as they navigate their religious beliefs within the context of their broader identities.

The interviews conducted for this study reveal the central role of religion in the formation and expression of identity among young Muslims living in the West. Religion, particularly Islam, emerges as the most common attribute participants use to express their identification. It is worth noting that the word count analysis indicates the frequency with which terms related to Muslim identity and religion appeared in the interview transcripts, further underscoring their significance in shaping the participants' sense of self.

However, for some young Muslims, their religious identification may be imposed or reinforced by societal pressures and expectations. They may find themselves labelled or stereotyped based on their religious background, which can lead to a sense of external imposition on their religious identity. This imposition may occur alongside their ethnic identity, creating a complex intersectionality of identities they must navigate.

It is crucial to recognize the agency and autonomy of young Muslims in defining their religious identity, even in the face of societal pressures. They actively engage in shaping and expressing their religious beliefs and practices, drawing from their own understanding and interpretations of their faith. This self-selected identification allows them to reclaim their religious narrative and challenge the misperceptions and stereotypes that may be imposed upon them.

3.5 Conclusion

Through the interviews conducted in the three countries, it became evident that faith held diverse meanings for the participants. Each individual had their own unique association with faith, expressed it in different ways, and attributed varying levels of significance to it. However, despite these differences, a common thread emerged: The majority of participants acknowledged that faith played a role in shaping their identity, morals, worldviews, and daily practices.

For many participants, faith was not a choice but something they were born into. It was ingrained in their upbringing and transmitted to them by their parents. The influence of the Muslim community on their faith varied depending on factors such as the proximity of the mosque to their residence and the level of involvement their family had within the local community.

The level of interaction with the Muslim community also impacted the participants' understanding and practice of their faith. Those who had regular contact with the community through mosque activities, religious events, and social gatherings tended to have a stronger sense of connection to their faith. They often drew support, guidance, and a sense of belonging from the community, which reinforced their faith and its importance in their lives.

However, it is essential to note that not all participants had the same level of engagement with the Muslim community. Factors such as geographic location, cultural background, and individual circumstances influenced their degree of involvement. Some participants lived in areas where the Muslim community was less visible or accessible, limiting their interactions. Others had families who were less engaged with the local community, which affected their exposure to Islamic teachings and communal activities.

Our results show that across all three countries, there are a host of views regarding Sharia. They highlight several important points about the varied perspectives on Sharia within the three countries and among different groups of participants. The study's findings indicate that there is a higher level of support for Sharia or Sharia-inspired allowances among the participants in our study compared to the study by Possamai et al. (2016), which reported only two out of 57 participants supporting Sharia tribunals. This difference in findings could be attributed to the generational shift and evolving views among young Muslims, as highlighted by Nilan's (2017) study in the UK.

This study also reveals that many participants in your sample believe that Sharia supports human rights, including women's rights. This aligns with the findings of Moghissi and Ghorashi (2016), who found that female Muslim participants viewed Sharia-driven family law as protective of Muslim women's rights compared to alternative state laws. These findings emphasize the nuanced perspectives on Sharia and its potential benefits, particularly within specific domains such as family law (Yilmaz 2002).

The influence of Islam as an identity, particularly among the younger generation, is a notable aspect of our study. The post-9/11 context and increased visibility of Islam and Muslims have contributed to the foregrounding of religious identity in the lives of young Muslims in the West. This suggests that Islam plays a significant role in shaping their views and considerations, including their perspectives on legal pluralism.

References

Moghissi, H., and Ghorashi, H. 2016. *Muslim Diaspora in the West: Negotiating Gender, Home and Belonging*. New York: Routledge.

Nilan, P. 2017. *Muslim Youth in the Diaspora: Challenging Extremism Through Popular Culture*. Oxon: Routledge.

Possamai, A., Bryan, S.T., Jennifer, E.C., Malcolm, V., and Selda, D. 2016. Shari'a and Everyday Life in Sydney. *Australian Geographer*, 47(3), 341–354. https://doi.org/10.1080/00049182.2016.1191137

Yilmaz, I. 2000. Muslim Law in Britain, Reflections in the Socio-Legal Sphere and Differential Legal Treatment. *Journal of Muslim Minority Affairs*, 20(2): 353–360. https://doi.org/10.1080/713680357

Yilmaz, I. 2001. Law as Chameleon: The Question of Incorporation of Muslim Personal Law into the English Law. *Journal of Muslim Minority Affairs*, 21(2), 297–308.

Yilmaz, I. 2002. The Challenge of Post-Modern Legality and Muslim Legal Pluralism in England. *Journal of Ethnic and Migration Studies*, 28(2), 343–354.

Yilmaz, I. 2016. The Nature of Islamophobia: Some Key Features. In: Douglas Pratt, and Rachel Woodlock, eds. *Fear of Muslims? International Perspectives on Islamophobia. Boundaries of Religious Freedom: Regulating Religion in Diverse Societies.* Switzerland: Springer, 19–30.

4 Young Legal Pluralists and Muslim Secularists on Sharia

4.1 Introduction

The interviews included questions specifically targeting the participants' thoughts and opinions on Sharia, its applicability in Muslim-majority countries, and its applicability in Western countries. These inquiries sought to explore the participants' understanding, attitudes, and utilization of Sharia as a guiding principle in their daily lives.

By posing questions such as "What are your thoughts about Sharia (Islamic law)?" and "Is Sharia law applicable in Muslim-majority countries?" the research aimed to gain insights into the participants' perceptions of Sharia and its role within predominantly Muslim societies. This line of questioning allowed for an exploration of their views on the significance of Sharia as a legal and ethical framework in Muslim-majority contexts.

Similarly, by asking about the applicability of Sharia law in Western countries, the research sought to understand the participants' perspectives on the compatibility of Islamic legal principles with the legal systems and social contexts of Western societies. This line of questioning aimed to uncover their thoughts on the coexistence of Sharia alongside the established legal frameworks in Western countries.

The analysis of the data revealed two main types, each with its own subtypes, representing the participants' views on Sharia (see also Yilmaz 2012, 2023). The first type, termed "Legal Pluralists," encompasses individuals who view Sharia as useful and advocate for its implementation. Within this type, there are two subtypes: Legal Pluralist A and Legal Pluralist B.

Legal Pluralist A advocates for the official implementation of Sharia within the legal system at a constitutional level specifically. However, their stance is that Sharia should be applicable only to Muslim citizens living in Western countries. They believe that incorporating Sharia into the legal framework would benefit society morally and spiritually.

On the other hand, Legal Pluralist B takes a broader approach and argues for Sharia to be a formal part of the legal system applicable to all individuals, regardless of their religious affiliation. They perceive Sharia as a beneficial framework that can contribute to the overall well-being of society.

DOI: 10.4324/9781003482604-4

The second type identified is "Muslim Secularists," which consists of individuals who do not believe Sharia has a place in the Western world. Within this type, there are two subtypes: Muslim Secularist A and Muslim Secularist B.

Muslim Secularist A outright rejects the principles of Sharia and considers it obsolete in the context of the modern world. They do not see any relevance or utility in incorporating Sharia into the legal system of Western countries.

Muslim Secularist B holds the view that Sharia may have a place in Muslim-majority countries but not in non-Muslim countries due to the religious diversity present. They believe that Sharia should be applicable where the majority of the population follows Islam, but it is not suitable for countries with diverse religious compositions.

It is important to note that while the participants had opinions on the issue of Sharia, a significant portion expressed a lack of proper education on the subject, leading to a less confident stance. Furthermore, many participants acknowledged the negative connotation associated with the term "Sharia" in the Western context, particularly in the aftermath of the 9/11 events. Nonetheless, despite these challenges, young Muslims still expressed confident opinions regarding the relevance or irrelevance of Sharia in Western countries and beyond.

4.2 What Is Sharia for the Young Muslim?

During the interviews, it became evident that many participants had limited knowledge about the concept of Sharia. When asked for their views, the majority admitted their lack of familiarity with the topic. However, this did not deter them from making educated guesses or sharing their initial impressions based on their limited understanding. They were open to discussing their perceptions and opinions, even if they acknowledged that their knowledge of the subject was incomplete.

On the other hand, a minority of participants chose to refrain from commenting on the issue of Sharia due to their lack of information. They recognized the importance of having a solid understanding of the concept before forming an opinion and preferred not to speculate or make uninformed statements.

Eileen, a participant from Australia, stood out as one of the individuals who chose not to engage in guesswork or speculation when discussing the concept of Sharia. In her response, she explained,

> Sharia law, to be honest, I don't know too much about to give a right answer.

Recognizing her limited knowledge of the subject, she expressed reluctance to provide an uninformed opinion. Instead, Eileen preferred to refrain from making assumptions and speculation and emphasized the importance of having a deeper understanding of Sharia before forming any conclusions.

Eileen's cautious approach demonstrated her commitment to being informed and educated about the topic rather than relying on assumptions or hearsay. Her hesitation to comment without proper knowledge showcased her desire for accuracy and a genuine engagement with the subject matter.

Aanadi from the US shared her thoughts but felt that she could be wrong; as she explained,

> I think Sharia is living by the Quran and hadith, like, as a whole society.

Bihter, from the UK, also guessed it to be derived from the life of Prophet Muhammad and the teachings from the Quran. Similarly, Muntazir, who lives in the US, also explained "his" view of Sharia,

> Sharia, from my understanding, is what Allah ordained for us. In this life, basically, how we live our life and what not and what are the guidelines, I guess, if you want to call it that. Of course . . . Sharia law is like a governing guideline system, which some countries might have, but Sharia here is something that I think everyone should have. . . It's more like a moral compass.

Sofia, a participant from the UK, expressed her belief that Sharia law is part of the formal legal system in her country even though that is not the case (Yilmaz 2000, 2001). Her statement highlights a common misconception and lack of clarity among some interviewees regarding the status and implementation of Sharia within their respective countries. She guessed that,

> Sharia is the Islamic principles, the Islamic laws. It's like how we have laws in England; I think we have Islamic laws as well.

The use of phrases such as "not sure," "in my view," and "I think so" suggests that many participants lacked a comprehensive understanding of Sharia and its actual implementation in their specific contexts. It indicates that their knowledge about Sharia may have been derived from various sources, including personal interpretations, cultural influences, or limited exposure to accurate information.

Sofia's belief that Sharia law is part of the formal legal system in the UK could stem from misunderstandings or misconceptions about the legal framework and the relationship between Sharia and the state's legal system (Yilmaz 2002, 2016). It highlights the importance of providing accurate information and clarifying misconceptions to promote a better understanding of Sharia and its role in different societies.

Imran, an Australian, also made an erroneous assumption about Sharia as he negated the idea of the Quran, mentioning flogging and death sentences.[1] He elaborated with some confidence,

> Isn't Sharia the law simply prescribed by Islam? Over time, it has been mutated by people to think that it is totally disgusting, but it should be just the words of law. There is probably much not wrong with it. A good example of this would be that stoning is said in Sharia law – I mean death – when I don't think that stoning is ever even mentioned in either hadith or Quran, in general. It is more of a tradition rather than a religious value. So, while it has been convoluted, it has been changed, to put it easier; I think there is nothing wrong with Sharia.

Zeeshan, from the UK, felt that Sharia was related to justice only,

> Sharia is the Islamic rule and laws for maintaining justice.

While others felt that Sharia had legal and personal dimensions, such as Nargis, who is British,

> It can be split into two. One side looks into the governing of society and rules of the society itself, like, looks at the personal rules, how to pray, fast, and carry out principles of the Islamic faith.

When a word count query was run in NVivo on the answers to the question "What is Sharia law?" words such as "think," "probably," "guess," and their synonyms appeared 64 times in response to this question. This shows the extent of uncertainty amongst the participants pertaining to the issue of defining Sharia.

Saleema, a participant from the US, and several others shared the belief that Sharia is a dynamic concept that evolves over time and is subject to various interpretations. This perspective reflects an understanding that Sharia is not fixed or monolithic but can be interpreted differently by religious scholars and individuals based on their cultural, historical, and social contexts.

Saleema summed up her interpretation of Sharia and its dynamic nature in the following words,

> I think Sharia is the way that we use it in this modern moment. Like, in the twentieth century and twenty-first century. I think it's a collection or

1 Flogging is prescribed as a punishment for men and women who commit *zina* (adultery or pre-marital sex) in Surah An-Nur, 2. While forgiveness is encouraged, capital punishment is also allowed in the Quran. Surah Ayah al-An'am 6:151 from the Quran discusses the issue of capital punishment.

> body of laws; it is derived by study of members of ulama like scholars, some of it, you know, coming principally from Quran . . . So, you have different laws governing different aspects of how people do things. Anything from something as simple as how to pray that if that varies, both among Orthodox Muslims as well as other Muslims, to how you break your fast.

By acknowledging the dynamic nature of Sharia and the existence of differing opinions, participants like Saleema demonstrate an understanding that the interpretation and application of Sharia are not fixed or uniform. This perspective contributes to a more nuanced understanding of the complexities surrounding Sharia and its role in the lives of Muslims.

Zia, also from the US, shared a similar opinion,

> I think Sharia is . . . . Yes, it's the laws and regulations and reference to or in reference to the Prophets' teachings in the Quran, but taking into consideration relevant aspects of the day and age that we live in. That's very important, I think.

Yasir, who lives in the US, used the word "fluid" as he discussed Sharia. Like many others, he was not sure of its definition but firmly believed in its fluidity,

> It's a fluid thing where it responds to the culture, response of the people, response to the time. It's not hard and fast and fixed. It also has to respond to what's going on with people. And in my understanding, Sharia, it does that.

Arben, who lives in the US, was more confident in his understanding of Sharia and, like many others, always felt that evolution was needed in the concept. He felt that not enough change was made, but at its core, Sharia is something that needs to be adaptable. The participant said,

> Basically [Sharia was meant to] reform backwards society into civilizations in my opinion, you know. And it is an evolving – not all, but in a lot of its aspects – it is an evolving practice, right, so I do not think it is a stagnant practice. And it makes a combination of, you know, some divine guidance and intuitions laws, but also it is not only, you know, the literal interpretation of divine guidance, in my opinion, as I said, it is meant to evolve with other aspects of society as well.

The recognition of diverse opinions among religious scholars regarding the interpretation and application of Sharia is an important aspect of understanding the complexity of this topic. Different schools of thought and legal traditions within Islam contribute to a diversity of perspectives on Sharia, resulting in a range of interpretations and practices.

The acknowledgment of Sharia's evolving nature also highlights the adaptive nature of Islamic jurisprudence to address contemporary issues and changing societal norms. This recognition allows for discussions and debates within Muslim communities regarding the relevance and applicability of certain aspects of Sharia in the modern world.

4.3 Legal Pluralist A

Summaya's perspective regarding the implementation of Sharia for Muslims in Australia reflects a viewpoint within the legal pluralist category, specifically Legal Pluralist B, who advocates for the incorporation of Sharia as a formal part of the legal system applicable to all individuals, both Muslims and non-Muslims, in Western countries.

In her view, Summaya suggests that since Australia has a small but significant Muslim population, it would be fair to implement Sharia to cater to the specific religious and cultural needs of Muslims. This perspective is based on the belief that Sharia can provide moral and spiritual guidance for Muslims and that its implementation can contribute to a more inclusive and accommodating legal framework.

She was not sure if it could become a reality but nonetheless shared,

> So, they [politicians] can't enforce Sharia laws, for example, but even if they are doing minor things that are in the right path towards Islam, that should be possible because Australia is a multicultural country. They should be accommodating to the Muslims as well in their politics.

It is important to note that the implementation of Sharia in non-Muslim-majority countries is a topic of ongoing debate and discussion, with varying opinions among Muslims and non-Muslims alike. Perspectives such as Summaya's highlight the diversity of views within the Muslim community regarding the applicability and benefits of incorporating elements of Sharia into the legal systems of Western countries.

Ameer's perspective reflects a belief that the ethical principles embedded in Sharia could potentially benefit not only Muslims but also humankind as a whole. He recognizes the universal aspect of Sharia's ethical teachings, which encompass concepts such as justice, compassion, and social welfare.

His reservations were explained as follows,

> For Muslims living in Australia, I think it might help – I wouldn't say we might benefit, I wouldn't say benefit – if we bring in any religious laws into a country that does not identify with a particular religion, that would definitely not help at all.

However, Ameer also acknowledges the challenges of widespread acceptance and adoption of Sharia within a non-Muslim-majority society. The implementation of Sharia as part of the legal system requires careful consideration of various factors, including legal compatibility, societal acceptance, and the protection of individual rights and freedoms. It is important to recognize that accepting Sharia within a secular and pluralistic framework should be based on principles of equality, non-discrimination, and respect for diverse beliefs and values.

Safdar's perspective reflects a nuanced stance on the formal application of Sharia law in the West. While he neither advocates nor negates the idea, he emphasizes the benefits that informal adherence to Sharia principles has brought to his own life and his Muslim community.

Safdar, unsure of fatwas, shared his personal experience as he said,

> We live in a non-Muslim country, an American country, a Christian country, so-called, and they [local Muslim imams] passed the fatwa saying that you can take out a mortgage on one home and I think one car, like a car loan, just to survive because it is very hard for you to survive in America without taking out a loan for school. So, there are certain things that they have passed. . . . I think I do agree that there are fatwas; maybe I should not, as I said before, but I do think that fatwas are important. Like I said before, I do not think we need that necessarily. I think if you understand the Quran or whatever . . . but I do see the benefit in them, and I do think they are important.

Safdar highlights the role of informal law, which is shaped by Islamic principles, in providing guidance and ease for his family in various aspects of daily life. He gives examples of how adherence to certain dietary restrictions, such as abstaining from consuming non-halal food, has made his family feel comfortable and at ease, even in seemingly trivial matters like eating French fries from McDonald's.

Furthermore, Safdar mentions how informal adherence to Sharia principles has influenced his family's financial decisions, such as avoiding interest-based loans and seeking alternative financial arrangements. This indicates that Sharia's ethical framework has guided their choices and provided them with a sense of security and alignment with their religious beliefs.

Safdar's perspective highlights the practical benefits that adhering to informal Sharia principles can bring to Muslim individuals and communities in the West. It demonstrates how individuals find personal meaning and value in integrating their religious beliefs into various aspects of their lives, including matters of consumption and finance.

However, it is important to note that the formal application of Sharia law within a secular legal framework raises complex legal and societal considerations. Safdar's personal experiences and beliefs should be seen as one perspective among many, and any discussion about the formal application of Sharia law should carefully weigh the principles of religious freedom, individual rights, and the overall values and norms of the society in question.

Jasime's viewpoint reflects the importance of inclusivity and addressing the needs of the Muslim community within a multicultural society like the UK.

She explained that issues of human rights are universal in their application, but things such as dress codes should be applicable to Muslims only,

> I think that would be one thing. In terms of the way women dress according to the Sharia law, I don't know if that would sit well with British politics because I know Britain as a country, so I don't know how well that would sit with the people as a whole in Britain. As much as I can say that it'd be great, there are a lot of things that are not ideal, or that might not be realistic. So, I think some of them are useful in terms of listening to the people, in terms of respecting them, in terms of human rights. Other things, maybe not so much.

She recognizes the value of listening to the concerns and perspectives of Muslims and creating an environment that accommodates their religious practices and beliefs.

However, Jasime also acknowledges the limitations of implementing all regulations associated with Sharia law for the entire population of the country. This recognition implies an understanding that a diverse society comprises individuals with varying religious and cultural backgrounds, and it may not be feasible or appropriate to impose specific religious laws on everyone.

Jasime's perspective highlights the need for balance and sensitivity in accommodating religious practices and ensuring the well-being of diverse communities within a secular legal framework. It emphasizes the importance of finding ways to respect and accommodate the needs of different religious groups without compromising the fundamental principles of equality, human rights, and individual freedom that underpin a democratic society.

Asifah's perspective aligns with the notion that incorporating Sharia-driven segments within the legal system can be seen as a step towards inclusivity. She explained her point of view,

> I think, obviously, the Australian government doesn't have to [implement Sharia for Muslims]; it is their choice if they want to because this is Australia. But if they would like to be, like, inclusive to and respectful to other Muslims and the Muslim community also – if they come together and ask the government, I think there should be, there can be a small section where, if everyone involved in the interaction is all Muslim and if they all agree to do it based on Sharia law because that is the Muslim way of doing things, then yeah, it would be good to add it to the law.

She likely believes that recognizing and incorporating elements of Sharia law into the legal framework can provide a sense of representation and accommodation for the Muslim community.

By acknowledging the principles and values of Sharia law, Asifah may view it as a means to ensure that the legal system is sensitive to the needs and beliefs of Muslims. This perspective reflects the idea that a diverse society should strive to create an inclusive environment where individuals from different religious backgrounds feel valued and respected.

Noor's comment about the implementation of Sharia in Australia suggests that the participants' discussions regarding Sharia were primarily focussed on the needs and concerns of Muslims within the context of their day-to-day lives. She explained,

> Well, I would definitely think [implementation of Sharia] would be very beneficial. Especially when it comes to respecting people's, you know, for example, you know, Muslims are very strict on their eating habits, so a lot of food that comes out that would be nice like halal food. . . . So, I think law in terms of foods and as such, I think that would be nice to see.

It indicates that the participants were not advocating for a radical shift in the governance system from democracy to the Caliphate system but rather expressing a desire for accommodations and considerations that would make their lives easier within the existing legal framework.

The participants, such as Safdar and Noor, who expressed support for incorporating Sharia-driven segments or principles into the legal system, likely see it as a way to address the specific needs and concerns of the Muslim community. By recognizing and accommodating certain aspects of Sharia, such as dietary practices (e.g., halal food) or financial transactions (e.g., adhering to Islamic banking principles), they believe that a more inclusive and accommodating environment can be created for Muslims within the broader legal framework. The idea behind incorporating these segments or principles is to provide practical solutions that align with the religious beliefs and practices of Muslims without necessarily seeking to replace or overshadow the existing legal system. It is seen as a way to respect and acknowledge the diversity of religious practices within a multicultural society, promoting a sense of inclusivity and understanding.

Salman was quite clear in his views about the issue. He felt that for Muslims, Sharia's implementation would bring benefits. He summed it up in the following comments,

> I wouldn't want to impose it on anyone, certainly, but I would say that, you know, it might be good to have. You know, within the Muslim community, if people want to live according to [Sharia], my take on this is . . . if people want to live according to those sorts of principles, then it is not a bad thing.

Nargis, who lives in the UK, felt that for the Muslim community in Scotland, aspects of Sharia were already in place. She felt that granting an *iddat* period to Muslim women was beneficial for the community, and she supported such measures. She expressed,

> Well, there are a couple. Like, Scotland has given, like, a three-month window after a divorced couple to, like, there are three months, and

> if the three months – like, this is in the Islamic law – if they want to get back together and then the divorce is just removed, that is same in Islamic law. Also, like, I have an Islamic bank account.

In a similar theme, Zulaikha explained how legal pluralism would aid Muslim women in the UK. She used family laws as an example,

> I am not saying all parts can be implemented or emphasized here in British society, but certainly some parts, for example, an issue I think that is very important is Islamic marriages in the UK are not recognized by the law, whereas Christian and Jewish marriages are, and that makes it very difficult for Muslim women to get their rights in marriage and divorce.

The implementation of Sharia within a secular and pluralistic legal framework raises complex challenges and requires careful consideration. One of the primary concerns revolves around ensuring that the implementation of Sharia aligns with the principles of human rights, gender equality, and the rights of individuals belonging to different religious or non-religious backgrounds.

Sharia, as a religious legal system, encompasses a wide range of interpretations and practices, and not all aspects of it are universally agreed upon. There are differing opinions among scholars and practitioners regarding its application and understanding in various contexts. Some interpretations may align with principles of equality and justice, while others may be seen as discriminatory or infringing upon individual rights.

4.4 Legal Pluralist B

Within the Legal Pluralist B group, there were differing opinions regarding the formal implementation of Sharia in the Western context and beyond. While all members of this group recognized the value of Sharia and its alignment with the ethical values promoted by Islam, there was disagreement on whether it should be formally incorporated into the legal system or remain as an informal influence.

Some members of Legal Pluralist B believed that formal implementation of Sharia would be beneficial, as it would provide a clear legal framework that ensures the application of Islamic principles in various aspects of life. They saw Sharia as a comprehensive code of conduct that encompasses not only personal beliefs and practices but also broader societal values and justice. These individuals advocated for integrating Sharia into the legal system to uphold these ethical values and promote a just and moral society.

On the other hand, there were members of Legal Pluralist B who felt that Sharia should remain an informal influence rather than be formally implemented. They recognized the potential challenges and complexities that may arise from integrating a religious legal system into a secular and pluralistic society. They believed that Sharia's influence could still be present through personal choices, community practices, and voluntary adherence without requiring formal legal recognition. They may see the informal nature of Sharia as a way to maintain religious autonomy and accommodate the diverse beliefs and practices within society.

Asher's perspective reflects a belief that Islam is compatible with liberal democratic values and that individuals can follow the laws of liberal democracies while adhering to their Islamic principles. Asher explained that there are some human rights laws he does not agree with but still chooses to follow the law. He explained,

> So, I do not think there is a need for a separate fique for living in the Western society because that is just like changing up religion. Islam is taught to be a very universal religion, and it needs to be seen that way.

According to Asher, Islam provides enough flexibility and guidance to accommodate the laws and regulations established by liberal democracies, as many of these principles align with the human rights and ethical values promoted by Islam.

Asher's viewpoint emphasizes the importance of respecting the laws of the country in which one resides, even if there may be certain aspects or regulations that an individual disagrees with. Rather than engaging in rebellion or breaking the law, Asher suggests it is better to find alternative solutions, such as moving to a different location or seeking ways to address concerns peacefully.

This perspective reflects a pragmatic approach that recognizes the importance of upholding the law and engaging in peaceful means to address any perceived conflicts between personal beliefs and legal requirements. It underscores the idea that religious individuals can navigate the complexities of living in a diverse society by seeking harmony between their faith and the legal framework of the country they reside in.

Liaqat's perspective suggests that Islam's universal teachings are applicable to all members of society, regardless of their religious or cultural background. Citing his participation in the Black Lives Matter movement, he explained,

> I think, just recently, it has been towards, like, the Back Lives Matters protests, and I think that is a very apparent example of America, which is, like, supposed to be an example of equity and justice and where it goes against that and it reminded me of the, like, Prophet Muhammad's final sermon where he said that "no Arab is superior to a non-Arab and no white is superior to a black and no black is superior to black," and that is one on racial lines, so Islam does say that even though the religion started in the land of Arabia, and even though many of the faith are Arabic, that does not mean that the Arabs are superior and it also does not that people who do not practice Islam, there should not be hardship for the people who do not practice Islam.

This viewpoint emphasizes the inclusive nature of Islam and its potential to offer guidance and ethical principles that can benefit individuals beyond the Muslim community.

By considering Islam's teachings as universal, Liaqat implies that the values and principles espoused by Islam are not limited to Muslims alone but can have relevance and value for society at large. This perspective aligns with the belief that Islamic teachings promote justice, compassion, and ethical conduct, which can contribute to the well-being and harmony of all individuals, regardless of their religious beliefs.

Indeed, Asher and Liaqat's viewpoints emphasize the belief that Islamic teachings can have a positive impact on both Muslims and non-Muslims in the US despite not advocating for the formal implementation of Sharia in the legal system. They recognize the universal nature of Islamic principles and values, suggesting that these teachings can offer guidance and promote ethical conduct that is beneficial to society as a whole.

Their perspectives align with the idea that Islam provides a framework for individuals to navigate their lives and make choices that uphold principles of justice, compassion, and human rights. They believe adhering to these principles can benefit individuals, regardless of their religious affiliation, and contribute to the betterment of society.

By not advocating for the formal implementation of Sharia, Asher and Liaqat likely acknowledge the complexities and challenges associated with integrating religious laws into a secular legal system. They may recognize that maintaining a separation between religious practices and the state's legal framework is necessary in a diverse and pluralistic society like the US. However, they still uphold the belief that the ethical teachings of Islam can positively influence individuals and society as a whole.

Arben's perspective suggests a unique interpretation of the US Constitution and its relationship to Islamic thought and Sharia. He explained his claim,

> I think US human rights mirrors [Islamic principles of human rights]. The West claims that they spearheaded the movement for human rights, whereas I think our Prophet and our Allah beat them to the punch a lot earlier. So, as rights of women go, a lot of legal issues, justice system-wise, you know. A lot of, you know, there is a wide range of fields that Islam revolutionized, you know, and the West kind of took from, I would say even, as I said before, the founding fathers [founders of the US Constitution] literally analyzed our faith and liked some of its aspects and said, "You know, okay, we can make this part of American systems as well," and I think it mirrors it. I think it is kind of a descendant of it, to be honest with you.

According to his viewpoint, he believes that the framers of the US Constitution drew inspiration from the guiding principles of Islamic thought (represented by the fiqh, or Islamic jurist) and Sharia when formulating the Constitution.

Salman's perspective highlights his belief that certain regulations in the UK, particularly those related to green spaces, have been influenced by Islamic law (Sharia). However, he also expresses uncertainty about this claim, indicating that it is his personal perception rather than a widely acknowledged fact. He explained it in the following statement,

> I have worked in property before, and there is a law in this country where, when you have a city or a town or something like that, if you have land that borders the city and to stop the other city or town from mixing with it. So, if you look at Northern Hampton and then you look at Birmingham, there is a gap, there is a land – a ring that goes around these cities, it is called green belt. . . . Medina and Mecca have this same farmland, this came from Sharia law, and it is part of this country! I am sure there are quite a few others, like, just in law and stealing and, you know, commandments of Allah, like not stealing and having some input in some of the laws in this country, I am pretty sure. I can't think it from my head, but I am sure there is something put in there

Najibah's viewpoint suggests that she sees the potential benefits of Sharia law's strict punishments as effective deterrents for crimes, which she perceives as lacking in the Western legal system. She explained this with the following statement,

> So, for example, in Islam, if somebody is a rapist, they would get hanged immediately, so they wouldn't have, like, as long as jail or something like that. So I think if we have that law here, there would be less of these situations, and for stealing as well, the punishment in Islamic laws is that they cut off the hands. This might sound barbaric, but it is there to prevent this from happening. So, if this was the law, then thieves wouldn't steal anything, but the law is here that if the thief comes to your house and gets injured, then you can get sued. I mean, he shouldn't be in our house in the first place, but then if he gets injured, it is our fault!

Aarish felt that Sharia-inspired financial systems are a cure for the current economic problems being faced in the West. She explained,

> Yeah, definitely. I think Islamic finance is very, very good. I think if that were to be implemented in British politics, it would help the economy. So, for example, the distribution of wealth among the poor and the rich, the disparity, how I talked about poverty. We all know that there's enough wealth on the Earth to cover the whole human population, but the problem is the distribution. That is why we have the rich and poor.

It must be noted that many participants based their understanding of Sharia on their broader understanding of Islamic teachings, values, and ethics rather than on a comprehensive knowledge of fiqh (Islamic jurisprudence) or the technicalities of Sharia law. This highlights the importance of distinguishing between the theological and ethical aspects of Islam and the legal framework of Sharia.

Sharia encompasses a wide range of principles and guidelines that Muslims strive to follow in their personal and communal lives. It covers various aspects, including personal morality, family law, contractual agreements, and more. While some principles and values within Sharia may align with universal ethical values, applying Sharia law within a legal system requires a more nuanced understanding of fiqh and legal interpretations.

It is common for individuals to have a general understanding of the ethical teachings and principles of their faith without delving into the intricacies of legal doctrines. This is especially true in multicultural societies where Muslims come from diverse cultural backgrounds and may have varying levels of familiarity with fiqh and Sharia law.

This lack of sophistication is related in Amal's comment,

> I think if Islamic law was here, or it was used here, there won't be any poor people. I don't think so, because Islam says you should help everyone, someone in need, and you shouldn't leave anyone out, so I think Islam would be a good effect in Australia.

She did not have a Sharia policy framework to share, but it was more of a sentimental belief she expressed. Aqil, an Australian, felt that implementing Sharia would mean he could have holidays on occasions such as Eid. He further added that Sharia has "health benefits" for all communities, as it bars eating pork and drinking alcohol, which, in his opinion, leads to health problems amongst the Australian population. Akbar's idea of Sharia's implementation also came out as quite vague,

> [Sharia] would give people more sense of charter, more sense of faith. I think people would be more secure about themselves, etc. I think it could be even safer.

Zakria admitted that he is not a "scholar or anything" but still felt Sharia-inspired laws would benefit all in Australia. He also made an interesting remark, which shows how he felt there are "good" and "bad" parts of Sharia, and it needed to be "tweaked" to seek inspiration from it. This confusion about the concept was expressed in this statement,

> Well, it depends. A bill that advocates for chopping people's heads off if they steal, then not compatible. But if you are talking about the nicer

> things, like, you know, compassion and embodying that in law, then, yeah, absolutely, why not?

Noriya, from Australia, felt that Sharia was useful for humanity, but she also expressed her idea of "good" and "bad" Sharia. She used the examples of Saudi Arabia and Iran to discuss "bad" Sharia and explained that "*I think like to a degree* [Sharia can be implemented] *but not so strictly, so people can have their voice, you know,*" to show her support for its inclusion. Nilan, from Australia, also expressed the idea of Sharia having universal appeal and value. She felt that with the "right people," it could be beneficial for the whole of Australian society. Again, like many others, she confessed that her knowledge about the issue is limited as she commented,

> Because God loves everyone and wants the best for everyone, I feel like it will be really useful. It was used in the government. And it might rule out inequality, but it depends because Sharia is not a one-dimensional thing, and you need someone who is learned to look at it. You can't certify an outsider to look into Sharia law and make judgments about things. So, you need someone who understands Australian politics and the Austrian way of living and also understands how Sharia law works and how it can play a role in our society, yeah.

Hasnah's statement gives an example of "good" and "bad" Sharia, which were discussed by many in the Legal Pluralist A category. She felt that "good" parts were applicable and useful for all and "bad" parts should be forgotten. She explained it as follows,

> I wouldn't know, but when it comes to the rights of the women, I think they should take that page out of the Sharia law book, but in saying that, yeah, they wouldn't have equal pay in Australia, but in saying that I am not saying, "hey Sharia law and implement it in Australia." No, I am saying there are some things, some parts of the Sharia law, that are exactly what people are asking for without actually realizing that it is Sharia.

Anisa, who was born and raised in Indonesia and later moved to Australia, felt that Sharia, in her view, was "good." She justified its implementation for all Australians by saying,

> In Indonesia, we do have some Sharia. So, in Aceh, the government said to all the people, even though it is not they are not Muslim, the women should wear a scarf. So, in Australia, it is kind of hard. But if it is good for us, then I think yes. It should, we should, yeah.

Again, like many others, it is not clear what "good" really means.

The convergence and evolution of ideas within the legal pluralist perspective is an interesting aspect to consider. It highlights that individuals' views on the implementation of Sharia law can be fluid and subject to change based on their experiences, interactions, and further reflection.

In the case of Nargis, her initial support for legal pluralism for Muslims might have been influenced by the idea of accommodating and meeting the specific needs of the Muslim community. However, as the discussion progressed, she seemingly expanded her perspective to see the broader benefits of Islamic banking for all British citizens. This shift indicates a recognition of the potential value and applicability of certain Islamic practices and principles beyond the Muslim community.

She explained her views in the following manner,

> So, now a lot of independent banks are kind of starting to use that as well. So, I think there are definitely ethical things in Islam that can be adopted. I mean, just because it is Islamic, it does not mean it is non-Western or non-universal. Like these Islamic values, Muslims believe in anyway, you can live throughout any time in society.

Nargis' statement about the popularity of Islamic banking across the UK highlights how specific aspects of Islamic law can be embraced and integrated into mainstream society, providing alternative options and ethical frameworks in areas such as finance. This suggests that elements of Sharia can be seen as beneficial and valuable beyond the religious context.

These nuanced perspectives and shifts in views demonstrate the complexity of discussions surrounding the implementation of Sharia law and how individuals may reassess their positions based on further information and considerations.

4.5 Muslim Secularist A

Affan's perspective from the UK reflects a recognition of the progressive and liberal ethos prevalent in UK society. He explained his view as follows,

> I don't know if it will be justifiable to do that, let us say, un-Islam, if it would be allowed to do, I don't know if that would raise any complications. If it was doable, it would be, but I personally don't see that ever happening. I mean, even if it was to, let us say, if it does happen and if we were to implement it, we can't, because I feel like liberalism has taken up too much within these countries anyway. I feel like liberalism latterly shifted, like, already we are seeing more people who are emphasizing liberal thoughts and, like, empirical forms and, like, their own judgments rather than churches and mosques and temples, you understand. We have way more people . . . now in society, and it

> is becoming much more, as I said, liberal. People are kind of shifting away from religion.

He acknowledges the value of the principles and guidance provided by Sharia, which align with his personal beliefs and understanding of Islam. However, he also takes into account the practical aspects of implementing Sharia law within a pluralistic and diverse society.

His stance suggests that while he may find value in the ethical teachings of Sharia, he acknowledges the challenges and complexities involved in implementing it as a formal legal system in the UK. This perspective highlights a pragmatic approach that considers the realities of a multicultural society and the need to balance different legal frameworks and societal norms.

Affan's viewpoint resonates with the idea that individuals can personally adhere to and find guidance in religious principles while recognizing the importance of a secular legal system that respects the rights and diversity of all citizens. It underscores the notion that one's personal beliefs and the practical considerations of governance and societal cohesion can coexist.

Similarly, Affan felt that Sharia was useful for him as a Muslim as it helped him understand the practices of Islam, such as fasting and praying. However, he saw no value or practicality in its implementation in a Western country, even for Muslims living in the West.

Melek, an Australian, was not an advocate of Sharia's implementation. However, she did note that teaching Sharia as a subject to Muslims and non-Muslims would be a good idea to foster a clear understanding of Islam and the means to harbour interfaith harmony. She reasoned,

> It would not be all too useful because not everyone in Australia is Muslim. But it would be good to incorporate to educate people who are Muslim or even non-Muslims to learn the countries and what people have to abide by.

Eileen, an Australian, also felt that Sharia's existence for Muslims only complicates life for those living in the country. She was not in favour of the concept, and she said,

> I reckon everyone should live their Islam the way it is but also respect the Australian politics and their laws and not try to be like, "Oh you can't do this, oh you can't do that." If you are accepted to live in this country, then Islam, it isn't something that is trying to complicate your life. There are very open elements, and if the country says that you need to show your face if you are wearing a burka to the police officer, then you have to show it. Like, people bring it to such extreme extents that, "Oh, no my religion says this!" but Islam really isn't that, it is really making it easier.

For Jameelah, the Australian legal system was similar to the values espoused by Islam. Given the lack of good precedents for the successful implementation of Sharia, she felt no use for the concept. She elaborated,

> Australian laws are already set, so Islamic laws are necessarily set and implemented well. Like, it hasn't worked well in any country yet in the current climate, so I don't think there should be Islamic laws in any ways.

Latifah added to this discussion by saying she enjoyed the "choice" she had under Australian law. For her, Sharia law did not offer the same choices. She discussed Iran's example as she pondered the topic,

> There is some Islamic country, like Iran, like, they have got some rules that they say, you know, are based off Sharia, which I don't agree, and I am pretty sure even, like, in Islam, being covered for, like, every Muslim, even if they want or, like, even being non-Muslim, like, you know, Islam doesn't say you force Muslims, it is, like, a personal choice, give them that choice. Islam does not say force, but in Iran, an Islamic country, says that do it by force, I don't think it is a nice idea.

Fatimah was quite vocal about her anti-Sharia stance. She clearly declared it as irrelevant for this century,

> No, I don't think Sharia would exist, and I think Sharia law was made for a very particular time, and it was meant for, like, a world in which the entire ummah was Muslim, and that is not what we have, and it is divided, and so, like, it wouldn't even work, like, in an Islamic country.

Some were quite clear in their stance on Sharia. Kinza, who lives in the US, felt that, according to her knowledge,

> I'm not very educated on Sharia at all. So, I could be very wrong. But my understanding is that in Islam, you're meant to follow the laws of whatever land you live in as long as it does not overtly conflict with Sharia. So, based on that, if there is no conflict, I think the two can coexist.

For her, if the Constitution does not violate Islamic principles, there is no need to separate Sharia-driven laws.

The perspective of some Secularists, who believe in the spirit of Sharia but criticize its current state due to perceived moral degradation, reflects a nuanced viewpoint. They recognize the underlying ethical principles and values promoted by Sharia, which they view as beneficial for society. However, they express concerns about the application and interpretation of Sharia in contemporary times.

By attributing the perceived problems with Sharia to moral degradation, these individuals imply that the original intent and purpose of Sharia have been compromised or distorted over time. They may believe that certain societal factors or changes have led to a departure from the true essence of Sharia, resulting in negative consequences.

This perspective suggests a desire to see a return to the fundamental principles and values of Sharia, free from what they perceive as moral deviations or misinterpretations. It highlights the importance of upholding the moral and ethical teachings of Islam while also acknowledging the need for critical evaluation and reform in order to address perceived shortcomings.

Ajola, from the US, explained this view during a discussion,

> I believe that the first generation of Muslims was the best generation. And then every generation that comes, it's less than that, less good. So, I don't think that they're, like, two in order to really have the system applied properly. You need honest people, and I'm not sure if there are many of them left.

Nadimah's, an Australian, perspective reflects a belief that Sharia, as a legal framework, was intended for a specific historical period and context. She explained this narrative,

> I think when Sharia came along with the advent of Islam, people were tamed, people became more civilized, and that is what I think its greatest benefits were at the time. Now, I don't think it is applicable because we are globalized and we live in different countries, and I think that law is arbitrary now. I think that, well, not arbitrary, but values are arbitrary, like, we all have a common understanding about matters. There are some things that people always pick out, but it is not as much as it used to be before, I think it is more universal now, or it appears more universal now.

She suggests that the principles and teachings of Sharia, which may have been relevant and applicable in the past, do not necessarily need to be the basis for contemporary legal systems. Instead, she emphasizes the universality of morality, implying that ethical principles and values are inherent to all human beings regardless of religious or cultural backgrounds.

In Nadimah's view, the idea of universal morality suggests that legal systems should be built upon shared ethical principles that are applicable to all individuals, regardless of their religious beliefs. She implies that focussing on universal morality as the foundation for laws can promote fairness, justice, and inclusivity within a multicultural society such as Australia.

This perspective raises the question of how legal systems should balance religious teachings, such as Sharia, with the notion of universal morality. Nadimah's viewpoint suggests that prioritizing shared ethical principles and values may be a more inclusive approach that can accommodate the diverse beliefs and perspectives within a multicultural society.

Saleema's perspective represents the viewpoint of some Secularists who believe that Sharia has no place in the lives of both Muslims and non-Muslims in a secular society. According to Saleema, Sharia is seen as irrelevant and incompatible with the modern context, regardless of one's religious affiliation. This perspective may stem from a belief in the separation of religion and state, where legal systems are based on secular principles rather than religious doctrines.

During her conversation, she made repeated use of words such as "I am not too educated," "this is my view," etc., to indicate her lack of authentic knowledge of the issues. For instance, she said,

> The direct answer to your question about its utility for political, or whatever, and you know, outside of, I would say, no, we don't really need to look at it, not really. We don't need that. We don't need anything from Sharia at all. But again, I'm a layperson. I'm not a student [of Sharia].

Saleema's statement about Sharia having no place in the lives of Muslims and non-Muslims suggests a rejection of the notion that religious laws should govern societal affairs. From this perspective, legal systems should be neutral and impartial, treating all individuals equally without favouring any specific religious beliefs or practices. The emphasis is on maintaining a secular framework that respects individual freedoms and protects the rights of all citizens, irrespective of their religious backgrounds.

Overall, the views of Secularists like Saleema reflect a scepticism or rejection of the relevance and applicability of Sharia in modern legal systems, placing emphasis on the importance of secular principles and the separation of religion and state.

In a similar tone, Zakria shared that when manmade laws are good enough, what is the point of adding on a second layer of divinely inspired laws? He said,

> I don't see why we would have to go there [inclusion of Sharia law] when just manmade laws are good enough for us.

He felt it was a personal practice and a preferential choice for those who followed it.

Fizza, from a British citizen's point of view, never saw the "right" implementation of Sharia. The room for exploitation and precedents that have been set made her feel that the concept was unsuitable for any place in the world. She explained,

> You know, so there is, like, some very versatile ideas in Islamic law that are implemented but it is not entirely implemented.

Later on, she contradicted this statement by saying that Sharia law could be an option as long as it did not contradict EU and UK laws. However, while discussing divorce and marriage laws, she reverted back to the idea that it is nearly impossible to apply in the UK.

Raina also added to the discussion by highlighting how, growing up, many young Muslims have no idea about Sharia. Even if were to be implemented, most would have no idea how to use it. The young Britisher explained,

> Honestly, I don't think it would be received well. For example, I don't think us young Muslims have a complete understanding of the Sharia law. So, if things were to be introduced, and I don't have full understanding of it myself, there wouldn't be a use to it. I would very much question it, and I think, generally, White people and Black people would question it too.

Saima discussed the same concerns and felt that in the modern world, even for Muslims, Sharia was just too "strict." She explained,

> Because I find it too strict for people nowadays. People today are very much not as before, as they might find Sharia very harsh. Even though I am not very informed, me saying this thing, but this is how it is.

Omar said the same thing,

> The conservative views and perspectives that a lot of people in the West would just brush off because, you know, what might be permitted for us or not be permitted for us might be permitted to them. So, I do think it is a really . . . worrying thing. I wouldn't want to live under Sharia law.

4.6 Muslim Secularist B

Muslim Secularist B mostly saw Sharia as useful for Muslim-majority communities. This did not mean that, in all cases, they did not see Sharia as irrelevant to their lives. It was the formal implementation that they saw as problematic in non-Muslim-majority countries. Another cohort felt that Sharia, for them, was not of personal use.

Hasan from Australia felt that, in an ideal world, Sharia would bring peace to Australia or any country where it is implemented. However, the interviewees implied that it is more suited for Muslim-majority countries because it would be impractical in a country like Australia, where most of the population does not identify with Islam.

Hasan explained this in the following manner,

> I think it should happen [implementation of Sharia law] because it would bring more peace to the country. I mean, Sharia law basically

> teaches us peace, how to be peaceful, and how to, like, control yourself, and it does apply to, let us say, a country like Australia. I think it would just bring more peace into the country. . . . As I said, it would be hard for it to apply; I mean it would be nearly impossible because us Muslims in Australia are a minority. . .. It is not going to happen at all! . . . If we faced the truth, it is not going to happen because I believe that Sharia is about me, myself, as a Muslim, and what I can do to follow those rules rather than putting it into a country itself, which is not an Islamic country, so I think it is not going to happen. So, I think Muslims in Australia should take Sharia and implement it on themselves rather than outside.

Hasan's perspective as a Muslim Secularist B reflects the idea that Sharia may have some perceived benefits and positive aspects, particularly for Muslim-majority communities. He believes that in an ideal world, the principles and guidance of Sharia could potentially contribute to a more peaceful society, even in countries like Australia. However, he also acknowledges the practical challenges and complexities of implementing Sharia in non-Muslim-majority countries.

One of the main concerns raised by Muslim Secularist B participants is the issue of relevance and applicability in the context of a non-Muslim-majority country like Australia. They recognize that Sharia is deeply rooted in Islamic teachings and traditions, and its principles are intended to guide the lives of Muslim individuals and communities.

Aziz's perspective reflects a common sentiment among some participants who identify as Muslim Secularists. He explained,

> I think Sharia is the law of Allah, so it can be used anywhere. Because, you know, Allah kept these laws from our Holy Prophet's time till the end of the time. So they can always be used. There's no such thing that is not compatible in society, because it always will be compatible. This is how I see it.

He acknowledges the universality and timeless nature of Sharia, recognizing its principles and practices as applicable to his personal life and Muslim-majority countries. However, he sees limited scope for its formal application in the UK, particularly for the general public who do not identify with Islam.

Aziz's viewpoint suggests a nuanced understanding of the cultural and religious context in which Sharia operates. While he personally finds value in the principles and practices of Sharia, he acknowledges that the broader society in the UK may not be receptive to its formal implementation.

This type of viewpoint often emerges as individuals grapple with the tension between their personal faith and the broader societal frameworks in which they live. They may recognize the value of Sharia in their own lives and the lives of Muslims in majority-Muslim countries while understanding that its implementation as a formal legal system may not be feasible or widely accepted in non-Muslim-majority countries like the UK.

Fayrooz felt that Sharia law, by design, is meant for Muslim-majority countries, and they, too, can choose to integrate it into their system to design a legal system intended for it,

> Because Sharia law is only used in Islamic states and unless the country, the state, is Islamic, there is no purpose for there to be Sharia law. Sharia law isn't part of the religion that we need to follow; it is just part of the Islamic state law that needs to be followed, and if you are not living in an Islamic state, then there is no need for Sharia law.

Ameer, also from Australia, felt that it would be unfair to impose Sharia on a non-Muslim demographic. He noted that,

> Well, you can't put religions and laws and values onto a whole nation that isn't majority Muslim, so it won't work.

Many participants expressed a more receptive attitude towards its implementation in Muslim-majority countries compared to non-Muslim-majority countries in the West. This perspective reflects a recognition of the cultural, religious, and legal context within which Sharia operates.

Samira was very vocal in her opposition to the relevance of Sharia in Australia but was okay with its implementation in Muslim-majority societies,

> Why would you put Sharia law here? You should put Australian law. I don't think it will be a good idea to have Sharia law in a political context. It has already caused a lot of problems, and I am not a big fan of it, and if you go to countries which have Sharia law, like Malaysia and Indonesia, it is suited for those countries as they are majority Muslim countries. In terms of Australia, we have a more relaxed and Westernized view, and it would be incompatible.

Rahima, from Australia, echoed a similar idea during her interview,

> Because everyone has freedom to live how they want like that. What I think: If you want to have Sharia law, then go to your Muslim country. Like, you shouldn't be in a secular country if you want to follow Sharia law. You shouldn't force it upon non-Muslims like they have nothing to do with it. They are not Muslims, and everyone has freedom to live freely, and again, I just think we should just be tolerant with everyone and let everyone live the way they want.

Imran, who also lives in Australia, explained his stance on the issue,

> This is not an Islamic state. The definition of Sharia is Islamic law. To apply an Islamic law in a non-Islamic country does not make any sense. If Muslims want to follow Islamic laws, then they are free to do so. They don't need to force it upon other people living in the country.

This sentiment was also found quite frequently in interviewees from the UK. Rizwan, for instance, noticed,

> With all respect, I would say no because we are living in the country, and that is UK, and implementing Sharia law is not necessary, with all respect. Purely because we are not a Muslim-majority country; if the UK was a Muslim-majority country, then that would be a different scenario, but I think because we are in a Muslim-minority country, especially now, then again, the Sharia law should not be applied.

Some even questioned whether it is okay to have Sharia imposed in Muslim-majority countries. Anandi's perspective reflects a common sentiment among some participants who question the imposition of Sharia in Muslim-majority countries. While they may acknowledge the cultural and religious significance of Sharia in these countries, they also recognize that its implementation can be a complex and contentious issue. She said,

> I don't think that's something that is feasible or fair in a society that is not a Muslim majority. Even in countries that are Muslim majority, I don't think it's quite fair to the people who aren't Islam. But I'm sure there are people who would debate that to say that Sharia is designed to be fair to those people. But again . . . until it's in practice. I wouldn't know how to feel about it.

The concerns raised about the imposition of Sharia in Muslim-majority countries can vary. Some individuals may raise questions about the potential violation of human rights or the possibility of theocracy overshadowing democratic principles. Others may express reservations about the diversity of beliefs within Muslim-majority countries and the potential for discord or unequal treatment among different groups.

At the same time, participants like Anandi may acknowledge that these concerns and considerations do not necessarily apply to non-Muslim-majority countries. They may recognize that the legal, cultural, and religious landscape in non-Muslim-majority countries is different and that the application of Sharia may not be relevant or practical in those contexts.

Aliah, from Australia, also felt that Sharia was more suitable for Muslim-majority countries, but she also shared her reservations about that leading to the exploitation of minority groups. She said,

> If this kind of system for the Muslim-majority countries has been going well and has been benefiting the majority of the population, then I think it is good, but if it is more of the extreme Sharia, then that is something that needs to be changed, especially if it effects minorities or other religious backgrounds in that country.

Participants may view Sharia as more suitable for Muslim-majority countries because these societies have a larger Muslim population and a cultural and legal framework that is more aligned with Islamic principles. They may perceive that Sharia can better integrate into the existing systems and structures in those countries. Additionally, there may be a sense of familiarity and acceptance of Sharia among the population in Muslim-majority countries, making its implementation more feasible.

On the other hand, participants may see the implementation of Sharia in non-Muslim-majority countries in the West as more challenging and less compatible with the existing legal and societal frameworks. They may consider the diversity of religious beliefs and the principles of secularism that underpin these countries as potential barriers to the formal implementation of Sharia.

4.7 Stigma Attached to Sharia

The participants, both the Secularists and Pluralists, confided about the degree to which the concept was stigmatized. Some attributed this to the post-9/11 context, while others felt that Muslim-majority countries' extremist implementation of Sharia, in regions such as Iran and Saudi Arabia, earned it a bad reputation.

Eileen explained how, for her, the bad image of Sharia comes from countries that follow it. In her view, not finding a country with a positive precedent makes her question the whole concept,

> I reckon being labelled as a terrorist is one of the biggest problems. But mainly in the Muslim world, like, people being very greedy, like, if you get what I mean? It is more evident, whether I am being biased or anything, it is more evident with the more Arab countries where they don't look after their own people. It looks like they are being controlled by the White forces, a.k.a. America. Like they are forgetting what the religion and what the Sharia laws and what the Prophet brought; like, they are putting those aside and actually doing something that is off to an end and, obviously, these groups like ISIS and things being labelled on the Muslims.

Another major reason cited for this stigma around Sharia came from the rise of global jihadist groups. Hiranur felt that in the US, Sharia had earned a really poor image,

> I imagine their understanding of Sharia law is incorrect, especially with what is going on around the world with this terrorism and all those

> political groups that use the name of Islam, and they do evil things around the world. That is an incorrect perception about Islamic law in the United States. And that's why I'm saying if they read the Quran and its interpretation, the life of the Prophet, his stories from trustable sources, if they will, or the scholar's opinions, then they would have a very good understanding. And then they will then think it's negative that is influencing the societies and their politics.

Rania's analysis added to the discussion. She explained how Sharia is viewed as quite backward and, when combined with its association with terror groups, it became a stigmatized topic. Rania explained,

> I think we've got a long way to go. The word Sharia, particularly the word Sharia, has such a negative connotation within Islam, and I think anyone who hears Sharia or anything to do with that, they automatically think "terrorism, oppression on women," and I think we've got a long way to go before anyone would be even willing to accept. For example, our current mayor in London, Sadiq Khan, I think if he even mentioned Sharia, he would be out-ruled.

Ben, who had converted to Islam, felt that when he thinks about Sharia, thanks to the media's portrayal, he feels uneasy about the connection. He explained this negative condition,

> That term, implementing Sharia, is such a, even for me, it is a scary thing to say because it has such bad things associated with it due to the media. I mean, from my own personal practical definition of Sharia, it is already implemented.

Akbar echoed his concerns as well,

> Honestly, if the Islamic law was to come into British politics, there would be a huge argument, of course, in the UK, as most of the government is against Islam, really.

Yasir also felt that lack of interactions with Muslims in real life and media stories meant that,

> [White Americans] don't even know what Islam is beyond the headlines and the videos.

Taslimah also felt that the media had a key role in spreading this stigmatized image,

> It would not be accepted easily because Sharia law has a really bad representation. It is in the media generally that it is really oppressive, that it

> is restrictive, but if people do actually open their eyes to us what Sharia suggests, like I said before, it can easily be compatible with our [Australian] system.

Muntazir, who felt that Sharia inspired the idea of a welfare state, shared how Sharia is often misunderstood by average Americans. He expressed his frustrations,

> Like when I usually talk to Anglo-American friends, and I ask them what they think about Sharia, they talk about . . . that there is that in Islam, it said that if somebody is guilty or did something wrong, they can be stoned.

A smaller number of them felt that the lack of innovation in Sharia itself was the issue for its poor reputation. Yunis discussed this,

> [Sharia] is actually in the hands of people who interpret it. That is a very, very huge responsibility. It could be bad, it could be wrong. And I see it has a room, a capacity to implement everything, although I am not an expert, but I do feel responsible.

Rizwan also felt that the lack of innovation in Sharia combined with the political atmosphere has made the concept quite contested. A lot of people in the UK see it as a cultural threat. He felt it was rooted in a misconception of the concept,

> So, that is the said perception with people, "Oh Sharia law! Muslims are trying to take over our country," and do this x-y-z with Sharia law, but I think that is a bigger problem that is outside misconception of people who do not represent Islam at all. They have painted that picture and image in people's heads and minds.

The emergence of a stigma attached to Sharia during the interviews reflects the impact of various factors, including the post-9/11 context and the portrayal of extremist implementation of Sharia in certain Muslim-majority countries. These factors have contributed to the negative perception and stigmatization of Sharia in the minds of some participants.

The post-9/11 context has led to increased scrutiny and suspicion surrounding Islam and its practices, including Sharia. Media coverage, political rhetoric, and stereotypes have perpetuated a negative narrative around Sharia, often associating it with extremism and human rights abuses. This has resulted in a general stigma and misconception surrounding the concept.

Additionally, the actions of certain Muslim-majority countries, where the implementation of Sharia may be perceived as restrictive or oppressive, have also contributed to the negative reputation attached to Sharia. Countries like Iran and Saudi Arabia, which have implemented their own versions of

Sharia, have been criticized for their human rights records and the curtailment of individual freedoms.

4.8 Conclusion

The notion of legal pluralism extends beyond family law and inheritance issues for young Muslims in the study. Participants' concerns and considerations about halal food, dating, prayer, fasting, and financial matters demonstrate a broader understanding of legal plurality in their lives. This aligns with the findings of Nilan (2017) and highlights the significance of a "proper way to live" within the framework of legal pluralism.

The study also reveals the presence of secularist perspectives that oppose the implementation and relevance of Sharia, similar to the findings of Korteweg and Selby (2012) in Canada. However, the cross-country comparison in our study highlights that the majority of participants from Australia fall into the secularist category, while the answers in the UK and the US are more divided between the pluralist and secularist groups. The participants from the US also exhibited a clearer understanding of Sharia and its implications compared to those from the UK and Australia.

It is noteworthy that none of the participants from the legal pluralist category in our study saw Sharia as a means to replace formal laws. Instead, they viewed it as a source of universal or morally relevant ideas that could be borrowed and applied for all while making the lives of Muslims easier. In contrast, the secularist group considered informal laws, including Sharia, as incompatible due to their perceived outdated nature.

The stigmatization of Sharia emerged as a consistent theme among the participants, attributed to negative portrayals in Western media and politics. This finding underscores the need for nuanced understanding and challenging stereotypes surrounding Sharia.

The complex relationship between identity and religion among young Muslims in the West is an important aspect highlighted in our study. Despite their support for Sharia-driven legal pluralism, most participants exhibited a liberal approach to the issue. This reflects the nuanced and multifaceted perspectives of young Muslims as they navigate their religious identity within a Western context.

References

Korteweg, C.A., and Selby, A.J. 2012. *Debating Sharia: Islam, Gender Politics, and Family Law Arbitration*. Toronto: Toronto University Press.

Nilan, P. 2017. *Muslim Youth in the Diaspora: Challenging Extremism Through Popular Culture*. Oxon: Routledge.

Yilmaz, I. 2000. Muslim Law in Britain, Reflections in the Socio-Legal Sphere and Differential Legal Treatment. *Journal of Muslim Minority Affairs*, 20(2): 353–360. https://doi.org/10.1080/713680357

Yilmaz, I. 2001. Law as Chameleon: The Question of Incorporation of Muslim Personal Law into the English Law. *Journal of Muslim Minority Affairs*, 21(2), 297–308.
Yilmaz, I. 2002. The Challenge of Post-Modern Legality and Muslim Legal Pluralism in England. *Journal of Ethnic and Migration Studies*, 28(2), 343–354.
Yilmaz, I. 2012. Towards a Muslim Secularism? An Islamic 'Twin Tolerations' Understanding of Religion in the Public Sphere. *Turkish Journal of Politics*, 3(2), 41–52.
Yilmaz, I. 2016. *Muslim Laws, Politics and Society in Modern Nation States: Dynamic Legal Pluralisms in England, Turkey and Pakistan*. London and New York: Routledge.
Yilmaz, I. 2023. Muslim Secularism by Conduct: Attitudes of Young Australian Muslims to Legal Pluralism and Sharia. *Journal of Intercultural Studies*, 44(2), 274–288. https://doi.org/10.1080/07256868.2022.2104826

5 Seeking Sharia Knowledge

Imams and Other Sources

5.1 Introduction

This chapter investigates the evolving role of religious scholars, commonly known as ulama or imams, in Muslim societies. This topic has garnered considerable academic interest over the years, and recent developments have placed even greater emphasis on understanding the ulama's position and function within the context of fragmented religious authority in traditional Islam. Traditionally, religious scholars have held a pivotal role in shaping public discourse and providing moral guidance to individuals and communities in Muslim societies. However, the current era of religious authority fragmentation has presented new challenges for ulama and imams as they navigate changing social and political landscapes (Yilmaz 2005, 2016a, 2020).

This chapter takes a closer look at how the ulama's role in state-society relations has evolved over time and explores the unique challenges they face in the present context. It does so by drawing upon themes derived from interviews conducted with a younger generation of Muslims who have been raised in Western countries. By focussing on this specific demographic, the chapter seeks to shed light on the implications of changing religious dynamics for the ulama and imams, as well as their interactions with the younger Muslim generation.

The chapter explores the perspectives and experiences of these young Muslims, providing valuable insights into their engagement with religious scholars and seeking guidance on various issues. The interviews touch upon a wide range of topics, including personal matters like getting a tattoo, dating, and matters of ritualistic faith, as well as broader concerns such as financial transactions involving interest and discussions on political issues.

Moreover, the chapter explores the process by which young Muslims determine which imam to approach for religious guidance. It reveals that the selection of imams is influenced not solely by ethnic factors but rather by a combination of geographical and social considerations. Factors such as the imam's location and accessibility play a significant role in the decision-making process. Additionally, the chapter acknowledges that minority sects may have sectarian preferences when seeking religious information, while gender barriers may also affect women's choices in selecting imams.

DOI: 10.4324/9781003482604-5

The chapter also discusses the reservations that some participants expressed regarding imams. These concerns may stem from a variety of factors, such as a perceived lack of expertise or the disconnect between traditional religious teachings and contemporary societal issues. By examining these reservations, the chapter aims to provide a nuanced understanding of the complexities and challenges faced by religious scholars in engaging with the younger generation.

5.2 Religious Authority of Ulama and Imams

The ulama are not passive individuals but active agents who actively shape the religious and cultural identity of Muslim societies. Through their teachings and guidance, they play a significant role in promoting adherence to Islamic principles and values (Naqvi and Jafri 2018). As religious scholars and interpreters of Islamic law, ulama have a crucial role in ensuring that Islamic practices and beliefs align with the teachings of the Quran and the Sunnah (the traditions of the Prophet Muhammad). The ulama serve as custodians of religious knowledge and are responsible for guiding the community on matters of morality, ethics, and spirituality.

The ulama are not limited to being religious scholars alone but also fulfill roles as educators, social workers, and mediators. They actively engage with various social issues within their communities, such as poverty, healthcare, and education. This broader involvement showcases the ulama's significance beyond religious matters and highlights their contributions to the overall well-being and development of Muslim societies.

However, it is important to acknowledge that the challenges to the authority of the ulama differ across different contexts. The authority of the ulama remains strong in many Muslim-majority countries, particularly concerning family law and personal status issues. In these countries, the ulama continue to play a prominent role in interpreting and applying Islamic legal frameworks. Their authority is recognized and respected by the state and the community.

In contrast, the authority of the ulama faces greater challenges in Western societies. The Western context is characterized by a more diverse range of Muslim voices and a higher degree of state control over Islamic institutions. As a result, the ulama's authority may be subject to scrutiny, and alternative interpretations of Islamic teachings may emerge. This diversity of perspectives and the influence of the state create a more complex environment for the ulama's role and authority.

The post-9/11 context has significantly impacted the reputation of the ulama in Western societies. Cesari (2018) highlights the negative stereotypes and perceptions surrounding ulama in the Western context. Cesari argues that the role of ulama in countering extremism and promoting peaceful coexistence has been overlooked, leading to misconceptions and negative views about their role in society. She emphasizes the need for greater recognition of the positive contributions of ulama and their potential in combating extremism.

The negative perception of ulama has been further exacerbated by the perception that they are outdated and disconnected from modern society. The ulama's failure to adapt to changing times and address the evolving needs and concerns of the community has contributed to their diminishing reputation (Zaman and Hefner 2007).

In some Muslim-majority countries, the state has sought to control religious discourse and institutions, often leading to tensions between the ulama and the state. However, in the Western context, state-controlled religious institutions are less prevalent. Instead, various religious organizations and community structures exist which can contribute to the fragmentation of religious authority. This fragmentation poses challenges for the ulama in maintaining their traditional roles and exerting influence on state-society relations.

Within this context, imams play a unique role in Western societies. They navigate the challenges and complexities of the Western context while serving as religious leaders within their communities. Imams often act as mediators, educators, and community organizers, addressing social issues and providing guidance to individuals and families. They play a vital role in providing spiritual and moral guidance to Muslims, particularly in matters related to personal faith and religious practices.

Factors such as secularism, modernity, foreignness, and the fragmentation of religious authority all contribute to the limited role of the ulama in state-society relations in the West. Nevertheless, imams continue to play a crucial role in guiding Muslim communities and addressing their spiritual and social needs. Understanding the dynamics and challenges faced by the ulama and imams in the Western context is essential for fostering meaningful engagement and dialogue between Muslim communities and the broader society.

The emergence of new Muslim voices and alternative methods of knowledge production has been another significant challenge to the authority of the ulama (Saeed and Saeed 2013). The arrival of new Muslim voices, particularly those educated in Western universities, has also challenged the authority of the traditional ulama. With fluency in both Arabic and English, these individuals are capable of challenging the ulama's interpretations and presenting alternative perspectives on Islamic texts (Kaya 2019).

The influence of sectarian and ethnic factors is also significant in shaping the role of the ulama. It impacts their authority, influence, and the dynamics of knowledge production and seeking within Muslim communities. Recognizing and understanding these factors is crucial for comprehending the complexities of the ulama's role and their relationship with the wider community.

This diversification of religious interpretations and sources of authority has contributed to a more complex landscape within Muslim communities, where the ulama's authority is no longer unchallenged. The following sections of this chapter look at how our study either agrees with these findings or leads to the exploration of newer themes.

5.3 Imams as Sources of Guidance

The interviews conducted with 122 young individuals provide valuable insights into their experiences and decision-making processes when faced with moral dilemmas related to various issues, such as divorce and getting tattoos. These individuals, like many members of religious groups, found themselves in moral quandaries and sought guidance to navigate these challenges. Interestingly, the interviews reveal that most participants did not have a regular imam they visited for religious guidance. Instead, they relied on alternative sources such as books, online resources, and social capital to explore and seek answers to their religious questions. This suggests a shift in the traditional reliance on imams as the primary source of religious guidance.

Although going to an imam was not popular among the interviewees, it is noteworthy that most of them had directly consulted an imam for guidance at some point in their lives. This indicates that imams still hold a certain level of authority and expertise in the eyes of the community, and individuals may turn to them when they feel the need for specific religious advice or clarification.

Furthermore, the involvement of family members and friends in discussing and seeking answers to religious questions from scholars reflects the importance of social networks and communal support in navigating moral dilemmas. The community plays a significant role in facilitating access to religious guidance and serving as a resource for sharing knowledge and experiences.

Yakub, when asked about his visitations to an imam, shared that his consultation varied from a range of issues,

> It is more on the tattoos, more on the music, more on what I can see and what you can't see.

Another regular theme in terms of consultation imams for day-to-day matters was related to the permissibility to borrow from banks. Najibah shared how she once consulted an imam to ask whether it was permissible in Islam to work at a bank where interest was taken. Zia, from the UK, also asked an imam,

> Yeah, I mean, one of them was specifically about ethical funding, right? . . . Like, how you eliminate interest from our everyday working banking system.

Another common theme amongst participants from all three countries was issues relating to eating. Another theme that emerged across the continents was related to questions about dating and marriage. The most common theme, however, was asking questions about religious procedures, such as issues relating to fasting, praying, alms-giving, etc. Haya's statement showcases this,

> I've asked a lot of scholars questions about, you know, for example, [Am I] allowed to combine prayers? So, if I don't have an answer to

> something, if I don't have a book or something, I will try to ask somebody that I trust. And then there's lots of scholars that I think could give answers, and some scholars give answers for God. [I] trust them in certain things.

Aqil, who lives in Australia, shared how he consulted the imam about various faith-related issues, such as the use of Gregorian calendars. He shared,

> So, I was like. "Can we follow the same calendar," and he was like, "Yeah, we can follow the same calendar of this country, there is nothing wrong with it, but we must know when Ramadan is, when is Muharram, Eid," and all of that stuff. When it's time to pray and things like that.

Yezda, who lives in the US, while discussing her question for imams, showcased how varied issues were points of consultation with imams for young Muslims. She shared,

> Oh my god! Everything! I mean, some examples, I guess would be, you know, like, learning about, like, Shia, what if you get married to someone who is Shia, about hijab.

The participants' questions predominantly revolved around finding a balance between their religious beliefs and the laws and informal norms of the country they reside in. It is important to note that the participants' inquiries were not aimed at seeking guidance on breaking the laws of their homelands. Instead, they were seeking guidance on how to navigate and reconcile potential conflicts or tensions between their religious practices and the legal and societal framework of their country.

This desire to strike a balance between faith and the law of the land is a common experience for individuals living in multicultural and diverse societies. They aim to adhere to their religious beliefs while also respecting and abiding by the legal and cultural norms of their respective countries.

By seeking guidance, whether through imams, books, online resources, or discussions with family and friends, individuals are attempting to find ways to uphold their religious values and convictions without contravening the laws and norms of their society. These questions reflect a conscientious effort to engage in ethical decision-making and to navigate the complex dynamics between personal faith and the legal and social context in which they live.

5.4 Reservations about Seeking Help from Imams

The unique experiences and expectations of participants living in Western cultures played a significant role in their perceptions of and interactions with imams. Many participants expressed a sense of disconnect or feeling discounted when engaging with imams who took a more "traditional" approach to Islam. This sentiment was particularly pronounced among women, who faced specific challenges related to issues such as freedom to work or to choose a vocation.

The participants' experiences and expectations were shaped by the cultural context in which they lived, which often differed from the cultural backgrounds of imams who were educated overseas. This created a perceived gap between the imams' understanding of the issues faced by young Muslims in Western societies and the lived realities of the participants themselves.

For women, in particular, the desire for gender equality and the freedom to pursue their ambitions and career goals clashed with more traditional interpretations of Islam that may limit their choices or opportunities. This tension led many to seek guidance from alternative sources or turn to online platforms and social networks to find answers that resonated with their specific circumstances and aspirations.

Najibah shared how her local imam was a source of disappointment because of his views on women in the workforce. She narrated the story,

> I was joining uni. I had to take a break because of visa issues, but when I was joining, he consulted the imam, and the imam said that the girls should study something that has to do with community service, such as nursing. And I was like, are you serious? I felt that was a very sexist comment because you can't tell what girls should study and what guys should study because we have the same brains, so I think IT is pretty good because you don't really need to go outside to do any work, and even if you do go out, you can have some days at home, and you can work from home as well, because it is all on the computer. But I just felt it was rude to talk to the imam about my career.

Sohrab admitted that he sought the help of imams from time to time but made sure they had "libertarian" thinking. For him, living in the US meant that the imams needed to be aware of the context. He explained how he avoided imams,

> I generally try to stay away from Islamic, from imams in general, because . . . I like to have my own freedom to determine my own interpretations. And I just generally don't really like to trust my religious practice in the hands of another human being. Because if I'm a human, and especially if I study this stuff myself, like, honestly, then I should be just as qualified to make decisions for myself or someone else. I would not necessarily go impose my own conclusions on someone else. But I do like to follow it myself.

He also noted that on a lot of online platforms, many e-imams were against feminism, which, for him, was outrageous and did not make sense. In a similar vein in the UK, Zulaikha shared how she "did not like" imams and avoided going to them "*because a lot of the times they are sexist.*" Thus, for Sohrab, Najeebah, and many others, imams were quite disconnected from modern thoughts and times, which led them to avoid seeking their advice. Ajola's discussion also showcases how young Muslims living in the West prefer to seek guidance from someone who grew up in their culture. She explained why she preferred to go to an imam who was born and raised in California as opposed to someone who was raised and trained in a Muslim-majority country,

> I chose them because everyone on that committee is a highly educated and respected scholar. So, they're legit in my eyes. They have dedicated their lifetime of 20-plus years studying Islam. So, I trust their knowledge. I chose them because they're in America. They're familiar with the culture here. And there are certain things that they do here that they wouldn't do in other Islamic countries, for example, like, if you want to buy a home. What should I do? Should I? You can't buy a home without the mortgage. Nobody has the entire cash-down approach. So, what should we do in that regard? For example, for me, travelling with a saved group, like in certain countries, Muslim countries, women might not be allowed to travel without having a male, my harem companion, with them from their family. But in the West, I mean, that's impossible to do because, you know, like all the male family members, they're working, and they don't have time over time. I need to travel somewhere and to see my parents to come with me. So that's something that they get it, like, what do I do in this situation, knowing that's how the conditions of how safe it is to fly will come back and, like, knowing the life here, that they will give me advice based on that, not just the trick, like certain rulings that are taken directly from text but without the context of it.

The participants' preference for imams or sources that could relate to their unique challenges and experiences is indicative of the importance they placed on finding guidance that resonated with their lived realities. They sought imams who could understand and address the specific cultural and societal dynamics they faced in Western countries.

It is worth noting that not all imams educated overseas necessarily lack an understanding of the issues faced by young Muslims in Western cultures. However, the perception among some participants was that imams with overseas education might be more rooted in traditional interpretations and less attuned to the realities and concerns of young Muslims living in Western societies.

These observations highlight the importance of creating spaces within Muslim communities where young people, both men and women, can have their voices heard and their unique challenges addressed. It also underscores the need for imams and religious leaders to engage with and understand the diverse experiences and expectations of their congregations, particularly those living in Western contexts, to provide guidance that is relevant, relatable, and supportive.

5.5 Knowledge Seeking Beyond Imams

Many young Muslims freely consulted scholars of Islam who were working at universities. Yunis, like some others in the interviews, went beyond conventional mosque imams. Yunis, from Australia, explained that, for him, anyone who was educated formally in the domain or had an esteemed position would be a consulting point for faith-related matters. He summed up,

> Someone who is respected in this community, religiously. And another would be some theological professor in leading universities to answer opinions and views.

Adeelah, who grew up in Indonesia and later moved to Australia, said an important point of consolation was people in Indonesia or the knowledgeable friends from her community. These "friends" were not formally educated but, in her words, were "seniors" of hers who had been in Australia for some time. Tasneem also shared a similar experience. She shared how she consulted a well-informed connection to get some advice about zakat. The young participant added,

> Oh! Yeah, I kind of, like, have a relative who is a family friend who has kind of, like, memorized the Quran, and he knows well about religion, and we have kind of asked.

Rahima, who lives in Australia, relied on her brothers and father for guidance. In her opinion, they were well-versed in Islam and credible sources, and they were non-judgmental as well due to the sometimes controversial nature of her questions. She explained her point,

> Yeah, I asked my dad, like, me and my brothers asked our dad questions all the time. Like, actually, my brother is, like, always having a debate about different things, and the good thing about my dad is that he will explain things, you know, in a logical manner. He will never get angry; it can be the most controversial question, and he won't get angry and will always try and explain it. And if he doesn't know, he will always go and research, and he will always ask us to go and research, he always asks us to ask questions, and I ask him questions all the time.

The choice to consult an imam over other sources was also determined by convenience. Many explained that, for some simple questions, a relative or Google might be able to help them. Rizwan, a Britisher, explained this point during his interview,

> Depending on the question . . . I maybe ask an Imam a few questions, and I just may do my own research as well by Googling it, or I have a

> cousin who is quite knowledgeable, and he used to be an imam in Pakistan, and he has come to the UK, and he does not practice the imam-ship here, but he is very knowledgeable. If I have any questions, to be honest, or if I am stuck. So, there are avenues that I would explore in that sense.

Sana, also from the UK, felt similarly and argued that, for her, asking questions online was quicker and easier because,

> I think it's really hard going to an Imam and asking them what the Islamic way is of doing it.

Sometimes, participants revealed that they might ask an imam a question via a friend or a family member. Rania from the UK explained how this worked for her when she needed clarification,

> Personally, I don't have any relation with an Imam, so I would turn to a friend who is more knowledgeable and has a Sheikh. So, I'll ask them, and they'll ask someone else, so it's a very long process, but I would eventually find out the answers.

In Australia, Salimah also opted for a similar approach to asking friends and family to consult an imam on her behalf. She explained how she went about this process,

> Usually through someone who I know is a bit more practicing than me. So, like, I have a lot of friends, actually, there is a lot of gathers and stuff that happen in some community, so I will just probably message them and take me to talk to an imam, or could you let me know? So, like, I would say they are more connected, and I get information by that person going and contacting that imam.

For Alimah and her friends, reaching logical conclusions together was enough. She confessed to never asking imams or another source. She felt confident enough that consulting amongst friends met her needs for answering faith-related questions.

This vetting process was mostly based on a self-constructed model of "logic" – basically what makes sense for the interviewee. Latifah, from Australia, explained it,

> Yes, it is the people that I believe in, and I trust them to ask, not every single imam. I don't read every single book by everyone, so it is particular scholars that I trust, so I read from there.

Jameelah explained how she trained herself to be aware of untrustworthy sources on online platforms, which enabled her to seek help online for religious queries. She expressed,

> I have educated myself enough to know, like, I know something is wrong, that is also why I can rely online, not because it is reliable, but I know I can know enough background and context to be able to say that "Oh, this is wrong" and "Oh, this makes sense." So, I have to read it, and then I have to make sure that I know, and I look at a few other sources.

Majeed, also an Australian, explained that one of his uncles was "kind of" an expert on faith, and he read books recommended by him for spiritual guidance and matters related to faith,

> I mainly get my books overseas from Singapore. They have English versions there. My uncle is kind of like an imam, and he has a bookstore in Singapore, and he can recommend titles, and some books here in Dandenong Plaza are from Singapore. I just go there and get them.

During the interviews, it became evident that many participants placed great importance on vetting the authority of the sources they consulted for guidance. Whether they sought answers from books, online resources, or individuals, they recognized the need to critically assess the credibility and reliability of the information they received.

Vetting the authority of the source is a crucial step in seeking religious guidance, as it ensures that the information aligns with their beliefs and is based on reliable and accurate interpretations of religious teachings. Participants were aware that not all sources are equally qualified or trustworthy, and they took it upon themselves to evaluate the authenticity and expertise of the sources they relied on.

When consulting books or online resources, participants considered factors such as the reputation and qualifications of the authors, the consensus or acceptance of the information within the religious community, and the adherence to established religious principles and interpretations. They sought sources that were recognized and respected within their religious tradition, giving them confidence in the information they received.

Similarly, when seeking guidance from individuals, participants were careful in selecting reliable and knowledgeable scholars or trusted individuals within their community. They valued the credentials, reputation, and level of religious education of the individuals they consulted, ensuring they were seeking advice from qualified sources.

By vetting the authority of the source, participants aimed to make informed decisions and avoid potential misinterpretations or misguidance. This approach reflects their commitment to engaging with reliable and trustworthy sources of religious guidance, enabling them to navigate the moral and ethical complexities they encountered while upholding their faith.

5.6 Sectarian Influences

The impact of the imam's sectarian outlook on the participants' perceptions varied depending on their own sectarian affiliations. Among Sunni Muslim respondents, the sectarian outlook of the imam did not appear to be a significant factor. This suggests that they were more open to seeking guidance from imams regardless of their specific sectarian background.

However, for groups such as Shias and particularly Ahmadiyyas, the sectarian identity of the imam became an important consideration. The participants from these sectarian groups may have sought imams who shared their specific beliefs and interpretations of Islam. This is likely due to the desire to receive guidance that aligns with their sectarian perspectives and addresses their unique religious concerns.

The importance placed on the imam's sectarian outlook by participants from Shias and Ahmadiyyas reflects the significance of sectarian identity and the specific religious doctrines and practices associated with these sects. It also highlights the role of sectarian differences in shaping individuals' preferences for religious leaders who share their particular sectarian background and can provide guidance that is in line with their specific beliefs and traditions.

These findings underscore the significance of sectarian considerations within the Muslim community and how they can influence the choices individuals make when seeking religious guidance. It also highlights the diversity within the Muslim community, with different sects often having distinct religious perspectives, practices, and sources of authority.

It is important to note that these observations are based on the experiences and perspectives of the participants in the specific context of their interviews. Individual experiences and preferences can vary, and not all individuals within a particular sect may prioritize the sectarian identity of the imam in the same way.

Salman, who had converted to Shia Islam, preferred going to the imam at the local mosque in his area. He described him as follows,

> He [the imam] is studying in Najam [referring to religious school], and he is a proper Shia scholar. I actually have his number. I think he mentioned he was from Pakistan, but he grew up in the US.

Indeed, the choice of mosques and the location where the young Muslims' families settled can significantly influence their access to imams who share a similar sectarian background. In the case of Nadeem, who lives in Australia, he referred to his local imam at the mosque, and it is noteworthy that the imam shared an Afghan and Hazara background with him. This suggests that Nadeem's selection of the mosque and imam was influenced by his desire to connect with individuals who shared his cultural and sectarian identity.

The settlement patterns of Muslim communities in Western countries often result in the establishment of mosques that cater to specific ethnic or sectarian groups. These mosques serve as community centres and places of worship, providing a sense of familiarity and shared experiences for the individuals who attend them. For young Muslims, particularly those seeking guidance on religious matters, going to a mosque within their sect can offer a sense of comfort and a greater likelihood of finding an imam who understands their specific cultural and religious context.

This phenomenon highlights how sectarian practices can emerge within Muslim communities based on factors such as geographic location, the composition of the local Muslim population, and the availability of mosques that cater to specific ethnic or sectarian backgrounds. It also demonstrates how mosques can play a crucial role in providing religious guidance and fostering a sense of community among young Muslims by connecting them with imams who share their cultural and sectarian backgrounds.

Ashar, who was born in the US and lived there, belonged to the Ahmadiyya community. The sect is usually outcasted by mainstream Sunnis and, at times, accused of being non-Muslims altogether. This meant that for Ashar and others from this sect, going to someone from their community was much safer. He explained,

> And of course, every imam I ask [questions] needs to be from my own community.

Riaz, also from the Ahmadiyya community, felt a sense of connection and cohesion due to his religious identity, and he expressed feeling happy about being close to imams in his community,

> So, the biggest thing that I feel really blessed is that our community is very easy to talk to, and there are imams.

The preference for staying within one's school of thought, even within the Sunni community, can contribute to further segregation and a limited range of perspectives among the imams consulted. Shiza's experience in the UK highlights her dissatisfaction with many imams she encountered, whom she perceived as "outdated" in their approach, particularly regarding issues such as women's rights and adapting to modern times.

She narrated an example to support her point,

> To be honest, the one woman Islamic scholar I came across, and she was from the Wahabi sector of Islam, and I am Sunni, and I know there is no point in me going to a Wahabi person because I knew that I was going to disagree with everything that she says. How can I get any confirmation or clarification from someone who does not even pay the same as me, you know, and that is the main foundation? So, for me there was not any point of going and seeking explanation with someone who I know was not going to agree with me anyway.

Shiza's decision to stick to imams from her own sect reflects her desire to find religious guidance that aligns with her specific beliefs and values. This choice allows her to engage with imams who may have a more progressive or nuanced understanding of contemporary issues, including women's rights. By seeking imams within her sect, Shiza likely feels more comfortable discussing and exploring these matters, as they are more likely to address them from a perspective that resonates with her own.

Overall, Shiza's experience highlights the impact of sect-based preferences and the desire for imams who can address contemporary concerns. It also underscores the importance of providing a diverse range of perspectives and approaches within the imamate, allowing individuals to access religious guidance that resonates with their personal beliefs and the challenges they face in the modern world.

The tendency to stick to imams within one's own sect is not uncommon and can be driven by various factors, including a sense of cultural or theological affinity and the belief that imams within the same sect are more likely to understand the specific concerns and challenges faced by individuals within that sect. However, it is worth noting that this approach may limit exposure to diverse perspectives and hinder opportunities for cross-sectarian dialogue and understanding.

5.7 Geographical, Ethical, and Other Factors

The preference for imams who are younger, more connected, and can relate to the age-related issues and the Western context of the young Muslim participants reflects their desire for a sense of familiarity and relevance in religious guidance. This preference suggests that they value imams who can understand and address the specific challenges faced by young Muslims in their respective countries.

While the ethnicity and nationality of the imams did not matter significantly for most participants, their scholarly training and qualifications were important considerations. This highlights the participants' recognition of the importance of knowledge and expertise in religious matters. They sought imams who were well-educated and had a strong understanding of Islamic teachings, particularly in relation to the Western context.

The overwhelming majority of imams being male, as expressed by the participants, reflects the traditional and patriarchal nature of religious leadership in many Muslim communities. The limited presence of female imams or consultations with the imam's wife indicates the existence of gender-based barriers and expectations within religious spaces. However, it is worth noting that there are instances where female participants sought guidance from female religious figures, highlighting the need for diverse representation and the recognition of women's perspectives in religious discourse.

The dominance of male imams is also reflected in the online presence of religious scholars on platforms such as Instagram and YouTube, where women religious scholars are notably absent or receive little attention. This gender disparity further perpetuates the notion that religious authority and scholarship are primarily male domains. It is important to recognize the need for greater representation of women in religious leadership roles, as it can provide diverse perspectives and address the specific needs and concerns of women within the Muslim community.

The experiences of Hiranur and Habiba reflect the diversity and flexibility in the choice of imams among young Muslims living in Western countries. Habiba explained,

> I've asked [religious questions] of Yemeni imams. I've asked, like, Indian and Pakistani imams about different things about Islam. They were all here [local mosque], and it was a person.

Their preference for following online preachers, regardless of their national or ethnic origins, suggests that they prioritize religious knowledge and the relevance of the content over the specific background of the imam.

Nouman Ali Khan and Omar Suleiman, both mentioned by Hiranur, are well-known Muslim speakers who have gained popularity through their online platforms. Their ability to effectively communicate and address contemporary issues faced by young Muslims in the Western context has made them influential figures among diverse Muslim communities. Their popularity indicates that young Muslims seek guidance from scholars who can relate to their experiences and provide meaningful interpretations of Islamic teachings.

Habiba's emphasis on the viability of the visiting imam also highlights the importance of the imam's ability to connect with the local community. This suggests that personal qualities, communication skills, and the ability to understand and address the concerns of the congregants are factors that influence the choice of imams. This aligns with the desire for imams who are more connected and can relate to the specific issues faced by young Muslims in their respective communities.

Haya's comment also indicated that, for most of the imams, the place of socialization and education mattered the most. She called it "actual studies" or "correct education,"

> [I feel comfortable consulting imams if] they have the correct education and they've actually studied, then, so, I don't care what their ethnicity is or where they're from, if I feel that they've actually studied.

Rizwan's perspective, as someone with South Asian ancestry living in the UK, highlights a common sentiment among young Muslims in Western countries. His focus was on him being from the UK. He explained,

> He is from the UK, and he currently travelled to Saudi Arabia, I think before the lockdown, and he is stuck there, and he is flying back to the UK soon, so he is born and raised in the UK.

The emphasis is less on the specific national or ethnic origins of the imams and more on their ability to understand and address the unique issues faced by young Muslims in the Western context.

The need for imams who can contextualize the challenges and experiences of young Muslims in Western societies reflects the desire for relatability and relevance in religious guidance. This suggests that young Muslims are looking for imams who can bridge the gap between traditional Islamic teachings and the contemporary realities they encounter in the Western world. They seek imams who can provide guidance that is meaningful, practical, and applicable to their lives, considering the specific cultural, social, and legal contexts they navigate.

The sentiment expressed by Rizwan and others underscores the importance of imams who possess a deep understanding of the Western context and can engage with the issues faced by young Muslims in a way that resonates with them. This could include addressing topics such as identity, gender roles, cultural integration, and societal challenges. Imams who can effectively communicate and provide guidance within this context are more likely to be perceived as relevant and reliable sources of religious knowledge.

Indeed, the interviews highlight that young Muslims prioritize finding a spiritual advisor or imam who can connect with them on a personal level. While factors such as age group, Western upbringing, or similar journeys towards Islam can contribute to this connection, the interviews indicate that cultural or national boundaries are generally less significant in the selection process.

The emphasis on finding a spiritual advisor who shares similar experiences or backgrounds may stem from the desire for relatability and understanding. Young Muslims often face unique challenges and dilemmas specific to their generation and the context in which they live. Therefore, having an imam who can empathize with and relate to their experiences can enhance their sense of connection and trust.

By seeking imams who can understand their perspective and provide guidance that resonates with their lived realities, young Muslims are more likely to feel supported in their spiritual journeys. This emphasis on personal connection suggests they value a relatable and authentic relationship with their spiritual advisors, allowing for open discussions, guidance, and support.

While the cultural and national backgrounds of imams may still play a role for some individuals, the interviews indicate that it is not a prominent factor in the selection process for many young Muslims. The focus is more on finding an imam who can address their spiritual needs, provide relevant guidance, and offer a supportive presence in their lives.

Yasir felt that the imam he had the most interaction with was someone who shared and understood his background. He was a convert to Islam, so the imam's background was a point of connection. He explained,

> He was a convert from Oklahoma City. Also, he was qualified to be a mufti, where he had worked up before. He was a white American from Anglo-American.

During the interviews, Nilan, who lives in Australia, shared how she found female imams on Facebook who she followed and also met in person during their visits to mosques and cultural events she frequented. She shared,

> Zohra lives in America, and she is in Texas. I think her parents left from a Middle Eastern country, I forgot which one. Yeahm Um Jamal ud Deen is Australian, she is Anglo, she reverted.

It is important to acknowledge that access to female imams or religious scholars can vary depending on the context and the specific mosque or community. While some women may have the opportunity to consult with female imams, as in the case of Zareena, others may not have such access and may seek guidance from the imam's wife or other trusted female members within the community.

The example shared by Yusuf highlights a common pattern where male family members, such as fathers or brothers, may take the lead in seeking advice from male imams on behalf of their female family members. He explained,

> For a daughter, because she was getting divorced, so he would ask like a Sheikh like an imam. He would ask him about, like, what she should do, like, she should fill out some papers and stuff and, like, the imam, like, advised him to do some stuff.

This may be influenced by cultural norms or perceptions about gender roles and responsibilities within the family and religious context.

The experiences shared by Zareena and Yusuf highlight the pressing need for increased opportunities for women to have direct access to female imams or religious scholars, thereby fostering a more inclusive and supportive religious environment. Promoting gender inclusivity and addressing the gender gap in religious leadership are crucial endeavours that can contribute to a more diverse and equitable religious landscape.

This raises important questions about the access of Muslim women to religious knowledge. However, not all female participants felt shy about consulting imams. Noor, from Australia, explained how she regularly consulted the imam from her local mosque,

> I would see him after prayer, basically – imam in the mosque. I would pray there, and when prayer has finished, I would approach him and speak to him about these kinds of issues and seek clarification from him.

By providing women with direct access to female imams or religious scholars, religious institutions and communities can offer a space where women feel comfortable and supported in seeking guidance on matters that specifically affect them. This approach acknowledges the unique perspectives and experiences of women, ensuring that their concerns and needs are addressed within the religious community.

In addition to representation and voice, gender inclusivity in religious leadership also serves as a catalyst for breaking down stereotypes and challenging traditional gender roles. Female imams and religious scholars can inspire and mentor other women, encouraging them to pursue religious studies and leadership roles. Their presence challenges prevailing gender norms and fosters a more inclusive environment for all members of the religious community.

Furthermore, female imams and religious scholars offer distinct insights and perspectives on issues that specifically impact women. Their expertise can contribute to discussions on women's rights, gender equality, and the intersection of faith and gender-related matters, enriching the religious discourse and ensuring the inclusion of diverse viewpoints.

5.8 Conclusion

The study conducted in three countries provides valuable insights into the role of imams and their interactions with young Muslims. The findings of this study align with previous research by Mandaville (2007) shedding light on the significance of discussions with imams on political and social issues among young Muslims in Western societies. Contrary to assumptions of social isolation or Islamophobia (Yilmaz 2016b), the participants' engagement with imams was driven by a genuine curiosity to explore faith-related matters, indicating the continued relevance of imams as sources of guidance. This underscores the role of imams in helping young Muslims navigate societal challenges and encouraging meaningful engagement with the broader community.

Moreover, the chapter highlighted the participants' awareness of different opinions and sources of knowledge within the imam community. It resonates with the work of Alvi and Kazmi (2016), which emphasizes the importance of recognizing and respecting diverse religious narratives. Young Muslims in the study demonstrated an inclination to seek guidance from imams they found relatable, considering factors such as the imam's worldview, upbringing, and compatibility with the Western context. This finding expands on the existing literature by showcasing that the imam's familiarity with Western social and intellectual realities plays a significant role in attracting young Muslims seeking guidance.

The study also addresses the gender dynamics within Muslim communities. While it acknowledges the progress made by a new generation of imams in promoting feminist ideas, the findings suggest that more changes are needed. Many participants, especially women, expressed concerns about gender biases and limitations in accessing imams directly. Women often resorted to having male relatives or the imam's wife relay their questions or seek guidance. This nuanced perspective differs from Cesari's (2018) assertion that negative perceptions of ulama in the West are merely a result of stereotyping. It implies that the conservative views held by some imams on gender-related matters contribute to young Muslims' hesitancy in seeking help from such figures within their communities.

Ethnic and sectarian differences also emerged as factors influencing the choice of imams among young Muslims. While sectarian affiliation played a stronger role, particularly among minority sects, such as Shias and Ahmadiyyas, ethnicity was a less decisive factor. Participants in the study consulted imams from various ethnic backgrounds. At times, they coincidentally shared an ethnic background with the imams due to residing in the same migrant community cluster. These findings resonate with the research conducted by Curtis (2010) and Ehsani (2017), emphasizing the significance of ethnic and sectarian considerations in determining imam selection.

In summary, the study highlights that young Muslims continue to rely on consultations with imams for a diverse range of issues. The decision to choose a particular imam is influenced by factors such as the imam's outlook, upbringing, sectarian affiliation, and gender. It underscores the importance of imams understanding and addressing the social and political realities of the twenty-first century to maintain their role and relevance within Muslim communities. By remaining attuned to the needs and concerns of young Muslims, imams can effectively guide and support them on their spiritual journeys while enabling their active participation and integration into wider society.

References

Alvi, H. A., & Kazmi, S. H. (2016). The challenge of state control over Islamic knowledge in the West. *Journal of Religion and Society*, 18, 1–15.

Cesari, J. (2018). The role of Islamic religious leaders in combating extremism. *Journal of Religion and Violence*, 6(1), 69–92.

Curtis, E. E. (2010). *Muslims in America: A short history*. Oxford University Press.

Ehsani, K. (2017). The authority of the ulama in Islamic history and their contemporary challenges. *Journal of Islamic Studies and Culture*, 5(2), 19–33.

Kaya, İ. (2019). The role of the ulama in the democratization of Turkey. *Journal of Islamic Thought and Civilization*, 9(2), 28–45.

Mandaville, Peter. (2007). *Global Political Islam* (1st ed.). London and New York: Routledge. https://doi.org/10.4324/9780203358511

Naqvi, A. M., & Jafri, S. H. M. (2018). Reaffirming the role of the ulama in contemporary Muslim societies. *Journal of Islamic Thought and Civilization*, 8(1), 1–17.

Saeed, A., & Saeed, H. (2013). The Challenge of New Muslim Intellectuals to Traditional Islamic Authority. *Journal of Islamic Studies*, 24(2), 127–151. https://doi.org/10.1093/jis/ett007

Yilmaz, I. (2005). Inter-Madhhab Surfing, Neo-Ijtihad, and Faith-Based Movement Leaders. In P. Bearman, R. Peters & F. E. Vogel (eds), *The Islamic school of law: Evolution, devolution and progress* (pp. 191–206). Harvard University Press.

Yilmaz, I. (2016a). *Muslim laws, politics and society in modern Nation States: Dynamic legal pluralisms in England, Turkey and Pakistan*. Routledge.

Yilmaz, I. (2016b). The nature of islamophobia: Some key features. In D. Pratt & R. Woodlock (eds), *Fear of Muslims? International perspectives on islamophobia. Boundaries of religious freedom: Regulating religion in diverse societies* (pp. 19–30). Springer.

Yilmaz, I. (2020). Muslims, sacred texts, and laws in the modern world. In M. Woodward & R. Lukens-Bull (eds), *Handbook of contemporary Islam and Muslim lives* (pp. 1–18). Springer.

Zaman, M. Q., & Hefner, R. W. (2007). Contemporary challenges to the ulama in Muslim societies. *The Muslim World*, 97(3), 431–456. https://doi.org/10.1111/j.1478-1913.2007.00186.x

6 Seeking Sharia Knowledge in Cyberspace

6.1 Introduction

The utilization of the internet as a prominent source of religious authority has presented a notable challenge to traditional sources, particularly the ulama (religious scholars) within the Muslim community. This shift has resulted in a more diverse and pluralistic religious landscape, where individuals have expanded access to a wide range of perspectives and interpretations of Islamic teachings. While it is crucial to acknowledge the limitations associated with relying on the internet as a source of religious authority, such as the absence of regulatory frameworks and the potential for the dissemination of extremist ideologies, its influence has allowed Muslim clerics and online bloggers to disseminate religious knowledge to a broader audience effectively.

One of the significant advantages of the internet in the context of Islamic religious authority is its capacity to reach a wider audience and facilitate the dissemination of religious teachings on a global scale. Through various digital platforms, such as websites, blogs, social media, and online forums, Muslim scholars and influencers can engage with individuals from diverse backgrounds, geographical locations, and linguistic communities. This accessibility has broken down traditional barriers of communication and fostered an interconnected network of religious discourse.

It is important to acknowledge the inherent challenges and complexities associated with the internet as a source of religious authority. The lack of centralized regulation and oversight poses risks, as the online sphere may be vulnerable to the propagation of distorted or extremist interpretations of Islamic teachings. However, it is essential to recognize that these risks do not negate the significant role that the internet plays in disseminating religious knowledge. Rather, efforts should be directed towards promoting responsible online engagement, developing mechanisms for verifying the credibility and authenticity of online sources, and encouraging critical thinking and discernment among individuals seeking religious guidance online.

As internet usage continues to grow and evolve, it is likely to shape further and influence the dissemination of religious knowledge within the Muslim world. The internet has provided a platform for marginalized voices,

DOI: 10.4324/9781003482604-6

diverse perspectives, and alternative interpretations of Islamic teachings to be heard. It has empowered individuals to engage with religious teachings in a more independent and autonomous manner, challenging the traditional monopoly of religious authority held by the ulama. Therefore, the internet's impact on the dissemination of religious knowledge in the Muslim community is a dynamic and ongoing process that merits further exploration and analysis.

This chapter looks at the transformative impact of cyberspace on the knowledge-seeking behaviour of young Muslims in their quest for religious and faith-related information. With the advent of the digital age, the creation of cyberspace has provided a new and dynamic platform through which individuals can engage with and access religious knowledge. The chapter aims to unravel the various ways young Muslims utilize and navigate the digital realm to satisfy their informational needs pertaining to Islam.

In this context, the term "cyberspace" refers to the virtual realm created by the interconnected networks of computers and digital devices. It encompasses various online platforms, such as websites, social media, search engines, and forums, where individuals can interact, share information, and seek guidance on a wide range of topics, including religion.

The chapter focusses on the behaviour and experiences of young Muslims in utilizing cyberspace as a prominent source for obtaining religious information. It explores their reliance on digital platforms and the impact it has on their understanding and practice of Islam. One significant aspect that emerges is the ubiquity of "Sheikh Google," a term used to describe the popular utilization of the search engine Google as a primary resource for Islamic information.

The chapter sheds light on the diverse ways young Muslims engage with cyberspace to seek guidance and clarification on a myriad of Islamic matters. It discusses the ease of accessibility and the inherent convenience of using search engines like Google, which have become the go-to choice for many individuals when faced with questions about Islamic teachings. The accessibility and convenience offered by cyberspace have empowered young Muslims to quickly access a vast array of Islamic resources and perspectives, thus broadening their knowledge base.

However, the chapter also highlights the awareness among young Muslims of the limitations associated with online platforms. While cyberspace provides a wealth of information, there are inherent challenges in ensuring the authenticity and reliability of sources. To address these concerns, the chapter explores the measures and strategies adopted by young Muslims to validate and authenticate the information they encounter online. These include employing critical thinking skills, cross-referencing multiple sources, and seeking guidance from trusted religious authorities or knowledgeable individuals within their communities. Moreover, the chapter explores an unexpected theme that emerged during the interviews: The perception among some young Muslims that cyberspace demands them to present a positive image of Islam or utilize the digital realm for noble purposes. This reflects the sense of responsibility felt by individuals to utilize the online space to project a "good side" of Islam and counter negative narratives or misrepresentations.

6.2 Impact of the Internet on the Dissemination of Religious Ideas

The rise of online bloggers and social media influencers as sources of religious authority is closely intertwined with the changing dynamics of political engagement. These non-traditional sources offer alternative perspectives and platforms through which Muslims can access religious teachings and guidance and engage in discussions on political matters. The accessibility and interactive nature of digital media enable these online figures to connect with a broad audience, share their insights, and shape the discourse surrounding political issues. It is worth noting that this shift does not imply a complete displacement of traditional religious authorities. Rather, it reflects an expanding landscape where diverse sources of religious authority coexist and contribute to the formation of individual and collective religious identities. The evolving role of the ulama in addressing political and social issues demonstrates their adaptability and responsiveness to the changing needs of their communities. The internet's impact on information dissemination and consumption has been transformative, and this is particularly evident in the realm of religious discourse within Muslim societies. In recent years, the internet has played an increasingly significant role in the dissemination of religious knowledge. Muslim clerics and online bloggers have embraced online platforms to share religious edicts or fatwas, thus establishing a new source of authority that challenges traditional channels of religious authority.

There is a discernible shift towards seeking religious guidance and authority from non-traditional sources, including online bloggers and social media influencers. These emerging voices have assumed a critical role in shaping political discourse within Muslim-American communities. Evolvi (2021) sheds light on the transformative impact of digital media and social networking platforms on the dissemination of religious ideas and the authority associated with them. The changing political climate in the United States has played a significant role in driving this shift. Muslim Americans are increasingly recognizing the need for political engagement and the importance of their voices being heard in societal and political discussions. Consequently, the role of traditional religious authorities, such as the ulama, has undergone redefinition in Muslim-American society. They are being called upon not only to provide religious guidance but also to address political and social issues affecting the Muslim American community.

Scholars have highlighted the internet's ability to provide Muslim clerics and online bloggers with a broader audience and greater ease in disseminating religious knowledge. This shift has resulted in these individuals gaining newfound authority that competes with established religious institutions. A central argument in the literature is that the internet has empowered these figures to reach a wider audience and disseminate their teachings more effectively, consequently challenging the dominance of traditional sources of religious authority.

The rise of internet-based religious authority does not necessarily entail the complete displacement of traditional religious institutions and figures. Rather, it signifies a diversification of religious authority, where online platforms and digital influencers coexist with established sources of religious guidance. The internet's impact lies in its ability to create an expanded religious landscape, where individuals have a greater range of sources to seek and validate religious knowledge.

The emergence of digital spaces as platforms for religious engagement has attracted the attention of clerics, both as information providers and seekers. Nurdin (2017) examines the Indonesian context and argues that social media platforms have become significant sources of Islamic information for Muslims beyond simple Google searches. He suggests that official clerics should actively engage with these platforms. In the UK, Sisler (2011) identifies a notable increase in the use of online spaces by preachers for issuing fatwas and facilitating communal unity and dispute resolution. This trend has given rise to a distinct category of online ulama who operate exclusively within the digital sphere and gather substantial followings.

Weimann's (2011) study sheds light on the darker side of online fatwas and clerics. He reveals that radical Islamist groups in Western countries have exploited online platforms to propagate their ideologies and attract followers. This highlights the potential risks associated with unregulated digital spaces and underscores the importance of responsible and informed engagement. However, Whyte (2022), in a more recent study, offers a different perspective based on the experiences of Australian Muslims. He argues that these individuals view online spaces as a means to explore and navigate their faith independently, often referred to as "Sheikh Google" or "do it yourself Islam" (DIY Islam). Whyte acknowledges the significance of cross-referencing information and seeking second opinions through consultations with imams or knowledgeable individuals to navigate the online space and obtain reliable religious information (see also Whyte 2024).

These studies collectively illustrate the multifaceted nature of online religious engagement. While digital spaces provide alternatives to traditional religious authorities, they also serve as platforms for established clerics to disseminate their teachings. The use of online spaces for fatwas and Islamic information varies across different contexts, highlighting the cultural and regional nuances in the adoption of digital platforms. Moreover, the potential for radicalization and misinformation underscores the need for vigilance and critical evaluation of online sources.

Amin (2019) reports similar findings about British young in the context. The presence of online sources in line with traditional access to imams is thus symbiotic rather than a sign of alienation from traditional contacts with imams.

The democratization of religious authority refers to the shift from exclusive control over religious knowledge by a select group, such as the ulama, to a more inclusive and participatory model where individuals from various backgrounds can engage in the production and dissemination of religious knowledge. The internet has played a crucial role in facilitating this democratization process within Muslim societies. One key aspect of this democratization is the increased accessibility to information and resources. The internet provides a vast repository of religious texts, scholarly works, lectures, and discussions that can be easily accessed by anyone with an internet connection. This accessibility has empowered ordinary Muslims to explore and engage with religious knowledge independently, without relying solely on traditional sources or authorities. Consequently, individuals can form their own interpretations and understandings of religious teachings, contributing to a more diverse and multifaceted religious landscape.

Moreover, the internet has created platforms for dialogue and interaction among Muslims from different geographic locations and cultural backgrounds. Online forums, social media platforms, and virtual communities enable individuals to connect, share ideas, and engage in discussions about various religious topics. This digital connectivity breaks down geographical barriers and fosters cross-cultural exchange, promoting a more cosmopolitan understanding of Islam.

The emergence of online platforms has also given rise to new voices and perspectives within the Muslim community. Previously marginalized groups, including women, youth, and individuals from non-traditional religious backgrounds, now have the opportunity to participate in religious discussions and contribute their unique insights actively. This inclusivity challenges the traditional hierarchy of religious authority, which has often been male-dominated and conservative, and allows for a broader representation of diverse Muslim experiences and perspectives.

The democratization of religious authority through the internet is not without challenges and risks. The sheer volume of information available online can be overwhelming, making it challenging to discern credible sources from unreliable or misleading content. Additionally, the absence of centralized regulation in cyberspace can allow for the spread of extremist ideologies or misinformation, posing a threat to the integrity and authenticity of religious discourse.

Furthermore, the democratization of religious authority through the internet raises questions about the role of expertise and qualifications. While the internet provides a platform for individuals to share their religious knowledge and opinions, it can be challenging to assess the credibility and qualifications of online religious figures or influencers. This highlights the importance of critical thinking and discernment when engaging with religious content online.

One significant limitation is the lack of regulation and quality control on the internet. With the ease of creating and sharing content online, there is a risk of individuals with inadequate qualifications or unreliable perspectives presenting themselves as religious authorities. This can lead to confusion and misinformation among those seeking authentic religious guidance.

Another concern is the potential for the internet to be exploited by extremist groups and states for the dissemination of radical ideologies (Yilmaz, 2019). Berger and Morgan (2015) emphasize the use of online platforms by terrorist organizations like ISIS to propagate their extremist beliefs and recruit individuals. The internet's global reach and anonymity can make it challenging to monitor and control such activities effectively. Counteracting online radicalization requires collaborative efforts between governments, technology companies, and religious communities to identify and counter extremist content while safeguarding freedom of expression and religious discourse.

Despite these limitations, the internet has become an influential platform for Muslim clerics and online bloggers to engage with a broader audience and disseminate religious knowledge. Social media platforms, such as X and Facebook, have particularly facilitated direct interaction and communication between religious authorities and their followers. Magraoui and Bouziane (2017) emphasize the role of X as a tool for Muslim clerics in the United States to reach out to diverse audiences, share fatwas, and participate in religious discussions.

The growing reliance on the internet as a source of religious authority reflects the evolving nature of religious engagement and the changing dynamics of religious discourse. It is important for religious scholars, institutions, and communities to adapt to this digital landscape by embracing responsible and informed use of online platforms. This includes establishing mechanisms for verification, promoting critical thinking and digital literacy, and fostering collaborative efforts to counter extremism and misinformation.

In conclusion, while the internet offers opportunities for the democratization of religious authority and the dissemination of religious knowledge, it also presents challenges, such as the need for regulation, quality control, and addressing the potential for online extremism. By addressing these limitations and utilizing the internet responsibly, religious communities can harness the potential of digital spaces to promote informed and inclusive religious discourse while safeguarding the authenticity and integrity of religious teachings.

6.3 Sheikh Google: An Emerging Trend

Within the realm of seeking Islamic knowledge, the utilization of the internet, or "Sheikh Google," as coined by one of the participants, demonstrated varying degrees of reliance among the individuals interviewed. The participants from the three countries under study displayed a range of preferences in terms of their utilization and trust of the internet as a source of Islamic information. Regardless of their legal perspectives, be they Legal Pluralists or Legal Secularists, participants from all backgrounds acknowledged the significance of the internet in clarifying inquiries related to Islam or disseminating religious content.

The term "Sheikh Google" encapsulates the notion of relying on Google, a widely used search engine, as a primary resource for obtaining information on religious matters. This term was introduced during one of the interviews when a participant, Abdullah, was asked about his preferred source of information regarding religious issues. Amused by the question, Abdullah responded with a light-hearted tone, referring to "Sheikh Google" as his go-to source. This playful expression serves as a way to refer to the use of the internet for seeking answers to religious questions throughout this section.

By adopting "Sheikh Google" as a colloquial term, the chapter acknowledges the prominence of the internet, particularly search engines like Google, as a first choice for individuals seeking clarification on various aspects of Islam. It highlights the accessibility and ease of use provided by online platforms, which have transformed the knowledge-seeking behaviour of young Muslims. Rather than relying solely on traditional sources of religious authority, such as scholars or clerics, the internet has become a readily available resource to address their religious inquiries.

It is important to note that the use of "Sheikh Google" does not imply a dismissal of traditional sources or a complete reliance on the internet alone. Rather, it reflects the recognition that the internet has become an integral part of the knowledge-seeking process, offering convenience and quick access to a vast array of Islamic information. Participants acknowledged the limitations of online platforms and were cautious about verifying the authenticity of the sources they encountered. This suggests a discerning approach among young Muslims in navigating the online realm and highlights their efforts to establish checks and balances to ensure the reliability of the information obtained.

By exploring the reliance on "Sheikh Google" and the participants' attitudes towards using the internet for religious inquiries, this chapter sheds light on the evolving dynamics between technology and Islamic knowledge. It provides insights into how young Muslims engage with the internet as a source of religious guidance and the implications it has for their understanding and practice of Islam. Through a nuanced examination of their experiences, the chapter contributes to a deeper understanding of the multifaceted relationship between technology, religious authority, and the knowledge-seeking behaviour of young Muslims in the digital age.

The pervasive presence of the internet has made it increasingly difficult for individuals like Abdullah to avoid engaging with faith-related matters in online spaces. As Ameer articulated, the sheer volume of content related to religion that appears on his newsfeed and the active participation of his peers in online discussions make it nearly impossible for him to disengage from these digital platforms.

The widespread adoption of social media platforms and the growing online presence of religious communities have contributed to the integration of faith-related content into individuals' online experiences. These platforms act as virtual spaces where discussions, debates, and information sharing about religious matters take place. As a result, individuals like Ameer find themselves exposed to faith-related content, whether they actively seek it or not, simply due to the nature of their online interactions and the content preferences of their connections. The young Australian explained,

> There is a page, and it is a Muslim page, that I am a part of, and it is more questions and answers. So, they throw a topic out there, it is more like a forum kind of thing. I am a part of it, like, I could go in there and look at the latest topic and read about it or whatever it is. . . . Because we live in an era where everyone posts what they are doing online, and if you are not a part of that you feel like you have lost, like, what that person is doing.

The constant presence of faith-related content on Ameer's newsfeed reflects the significant role that online platforms play in shaping the information environment and influencing individuals' engagement with religious matters. The algorithms used by social media platforms, based on user browsing history and interactions, often result in the customization and personalization of the content displayed to individuals. This personalization can lead to increased exposure to faith-related content for individuals who have previously engaged with or shown an interest in such topics.

Furthermore, Ameer's mention of his peers actively using online spaces to discuss religious matters highlights the influence of social networks on individuals' online engagement with faith. The participatory nature of these platforms allows users to share their thoughts, beliefs, and religious experiences, fostering a sense of community and enabling the dissemination of religious knowledge among peers. As a result, individuals like Ameer feel compelled to participate in these online conversations, as they don't want to miss out on the shared experiences and insights shared by their peers.

The integration of faith-related content into online spaces reflects the evolving nature of religious engagement in the digital age. The internet has transformed the way individuals interact with religious information and participate in religious discourse. Online platforms provide individuals with a convenient and easily accessible space to explore, discuss, and engage with matters of faith. Whether through intentional seeking or passive exposure, individuals like Ameer find themselves drawn into faith-related discussions in online spaces due to the ubiquity of this content and the active participation of their peers.

Najibah, for instance, felt that, for her, the internet was the most obvious place to seek information on faith-related matters. When asked whom she goes to with her questions about faith-related matters, she said,

> Just Google; I just try to find the best answer, whichever.

The pervasive presence of social media in the daily lives of many young Muslims has created a natural inclination for them to engage with faith-related matters on these platforms. Even when they may not actively seek out religious information, their regular interaction with social media exposes them to religious content through posts appearing on their news feeds.

Social media has become an integral part of the daily routines of young Muslims, serving as a platform for social connections, entertainment, and information consumption. With the widespread usage of platforms such as Facebook, X, Instagram, and YouTube, these digital spaces have become an accessible and convenient source of diverse content, including religious content.

As young Muslims scroll through their social media feeds, they come across posts related to faith matters, including quotes from religious texts, reflections on spirituality, discussions on religious practices, and even religious events or sermons shared by their connections. These posts can come from their friends, family members, religious organizations, influencers, or online communities focussed on religious topics.

Passive exposure to religious content through news feed posts has an impact on shaping the perspectives and knowledge of young Muslims. Even without actively seeking out this content, they are exposed regularly to religious ideas, discussions, and perspectives that contribute to their overall understanding of faith-related matters.

Moreover, the algorithmic customization employed by social media platforms plays a significant role in presenting content tailored to individuals' interests and preferences. If a young Muslim has previously engaged with religious content or liked or commented on such posts, or followed religious pages or figures, the algorithms take these signals into account and deliver more religious content to their news feeds. This personalized content delivery further reinforces the exposure to faith-related posts, creating a continuous flow of religious content in their social media experience.

The integration of faith-related content into the everyday social media experience of young Muslims reflects the increasing influence and impact of digital platforms on religious engagement. It blurs the boundaries between online and offline religious practices, as social media becomes a space for individuals to express and explore their faith, share religious resources, connect with like-minded individuals, and seek spiritual guidance.

Affan, who lives in the UK, shared how he used Instagram in this regard,

> There are good aspects. On Instagram, you can just make a page and post daily; an Islamic reminder every day, and that is good because that not only gives rewards to the person doing it, but people who are following it, is really good. It reminds people of Islam by seeing it on social media. It benefits the Islamic community on social media.

In addition to serving as a platform for seeking information and engaging with religious content, the internet has also become a space for young Muslims to authenticate the statements and teachings of imams or other individuals claiming knowledge about Islam.

Traditionally, the authentication of religious figures and their teachings relied on established channels, such as local mosques, Islamic scholars, or trusted community leaders. However, the internet has provided an alternative avenue for young Muslims to verify and validate the information they come across, especially when it comes to religious matters.

With the vast amount of information available online, there is a need for critical evaluation and discernment. Young Muslims can utilize the internet as a tool for fact-checking and cross-referencing the statements made by imams or individuals claiming authority on Islamic teachings. They can search for alternative sources, consult reputable Islamic websites or scholars, and engage in online discussions to gain a more comprehensive understanding of a particular religious topic.

By leveraging the internet as a means of authentication, young Muslims can independently verify the credibility and reliability of the information they encounter. This empowers them to make informed decisions and form their own perspectives on Islamic matters rather than solely relying on the authority and interpretations of traditional religious figures.

Fatimah, from Australia, explained,

> I think I like to use the internet to clarify things that I hear people say about Islam because sometimes people claim a particular hadith means this or a particular imam said this, and they just say it because they have just heard it from other people, and I like to go on the internet to sort of see exactly what was said or even to clarify bits of the Quran because I think it is really good instead of just focussing on [what] one scholar says and then look at what a couple of scholars say and then want to take an average of that.

The emergence of online Sheikhs or scholars has become a significant phenomenon in the lives of young Muslims, particularly through popular social media platforms like YouTube, Instagram, Facebook, and others. These online scholars have amassed large followings and have gained popularity among Muslim youth.

These digital Sheikhs operate in a format reminiscent of traditional televangelism, where they engage with their audience through various multimedia channels. They deliver religious lectures, sermons, and discussions on contemporary issues that resonate with the experiences and challenges faced by young Muslims today. By addressing relevant topics and using relatable language and cultural references, they establish a connection with their audience and provide guidance within a contemporary context.

One notable aspect of these online Sheikhs is their ability to connect with Muslim youth by sharing similar backgrounds and experiences. Many of these popular speakers, such as Omar Sulaiman, Nouman Ali Khan, Abdullah bin Hamid Ali, Yasmin Mogahed, Yusuf Estes, and Khalid Yasin, either hail from Western countries or have lived there from a young age. This shared background allows them to understand the struggles and aspirations of Western Muslim youth and offer insights that resonate with their lived realities.

The popularity of these online muftis and scholars among young Muslims is reflected in their significant social media followings. Figures like Mufti Maneek (Ismail ibn Musa Men), with over 4 million followers on Instagram, and Nouman Ali Khan, with nearly 3 million followers on Facebook, demonstrate the influence and reach of these digital religious figures.

Aftab explained how he sought knowledge by following online mufti videos. He explained,

> I do not ask [imams] directly; I watch videos. There is this bloke called Israr Ahmad from Pakistan. He is sort of a Sheikh. The Sheikh that is from Zimbabwe, Mufti Menk.

Hiranur, who lives in the US, explained that, for her, the internet was a good source of information, along with books. However, her use of the internet was determined by statements issued by e-imams on various issues. She explained these e-imams as "people" in her interview,

> Well, not the website. Like, the people I follow, they do have their own websites, but they just post videos on their Facebook pages or they go to YouTube. And I just search their names, and I see what they recently have there.

For Imran, from Australia, some imams on social media were really authentic because they shared their personal journey of exploring faith. He gave an example,

> The internet just has all the information, it has shitty stuff too, but it is definitely my primary resource where I would get any research to begin with. My main resource for Islamic research has been just a couple scholars who I personally believe worthy, the way you put it. Specifically, there are some guys, like Muhammad Asad, who I think is an Anglo, I think he is French or maybe he is from Austria. He went to Saudi Arabia, he lived with the Bedouin society who still spoke the original Arabic, stayed with them over a decade, made loads of translations, usually with all citations. These are the types of people that I am happy to look to for insight, not the general people that you pick, nah.

Rizwan's comments showcase why many young followers admire e-imams and their influencer-like interaction with their audiences. The young British Muslim explained,

> Just about his life and how he became an imam, and people might have questions about, like, daily things like Ramadan, for example, he would

> do a Q&A session, like, common questions and posts, like, site Sheikhs, and recite recitation of the Quran as well. He may do questions, and he may do online courses and tajweed and pronunciation and things like that, and his content is quite valued.

Behlul, from the US, also shared that he knew those he followed were "authentic." The muftis that he followed had a massive presence on social media. He talked about them in the following statement,

> I search online, but I can't tell you, for scholars, that I take their perspectives. Arguably, one of them would be Fetullah Gulen; yet another one could be Hamza Yusuf, and another one could be Nouman Ali Khan, and the other one would be, what was his name? Omer. Something I don't remember the last name. But these are the first ones that come to my mind.

He added that, in addition to being authentic, following different e-imams enabled him to get multiple perspectives on issues. Behlul elaborated on the basis of his trust in these imams,

> It's not like a random group of people can write random things; they give answers with references from primary resources, giving different perspectives of different schools of thoughts, usually, so it gives me a larger perspective of what different opinions and what's more applicable in my context, etc. That's something that I enjoy.

Bushra shared that, for her, it was a matter of convenience. For instance, going to an imam was a time-intensive activity, whereas the internet was always present and at her disposal around the clock. She explained her use in the following manner,

> You can't access that information straightway [if you go to an imam]. Do you know what I mean? Like, if you wanted an answer at night, but you would have to wait for them till morning. So, at first, I would ask online, and if I wasn't sure online, then I would go to an Islamic leader.

For Yusuf, the convenience came in the form of getting newsfeeds with useful Islamic information as opposed to reading full-length books. The young Australian confessed he never read religious books; rather, he preferred Islamic groups or followed them for daily or weekly newsfeeds. He said,

> I don't really read those kinds of books, but I look at posts about religion on social media and stuff; that is what I mostly do.

Zubeida, from the UK, felt that imams were hard to approach for women, and, for her, the internet helped in bridging this gap. She explained how many questions she never felt comfortable asking a man were now answered for her due to "Sheikh Google." She said,

> I think in this day and age it is very easy to ask Google, and well, maybe that is not very accurate, but, well, they have got a reliable platform, but in terms of research, too, there's a lot you can do. Maybe because I am a Muslim woman who wouldn't necessarily want to go to an imam.

Hiranur, who lives in the US, noted that she never really asked any imam questions. She follows imams on online platforms to get answers to her questions. The youth explained,

> I sometimes listen to their speeches. Just get more information about it. Like, some of the issues that I was interested in when it comes to Islamic law. . . . Researching that, and I did a lot of research about the role of the woman in Islam and what rights she has. Stuff like that.

The experiences shared by Zubeidah and Hiranur shed light on the unique role of the internet in providing a platform for women to explore and engage with Islam in a way that may not be readily available through traditional means.

For many women, the internet offers a safe and open space to seek answers to questions and concerns related to Islam. Zubeidah and Hiranur mentioned they felt more comfortable exploring certain topics online because they believed that imams or religious leaders might not provide the liberal perspectives they sought. This highlights the potential limitations of accessing information solely through traditional religious authorities and the need for alternative sources that cater to the diverse needs and perspectives of Muslim women.

Additionally, the internet allows women to overcome barriers of shyness or cultural norms that may make it challenging to discuss certain topics with men. Hiranur's comment about feeling too shy to broach certain subjects with a man reflects the importance of providing women with spaces where they feel empowered to seek knowledge and engage in discussions about their faith.

Noriyah, from Australia, showcased how, apart from online muftis, just watching other Muslim women dress helped her explore "modest fashion." Essentially, it was her way of gaining information on how to style in accordance with Islam. She explained this in the following statement,

> I think it is good because it has built a sort of community, you know, on Instagram, like, especially, I see that there are Muslim females, you know, talking, and there is fashion out there that is catering for their needs and modesty, so yeah.

Noriyah's example highlights how the internet can also serve as a platform for Muslim women to explore and embrace their identities, specifically in relation to modest fashion. By watching other Muslim women dress and style themselves in accordance with Islamic principles, Noriyah was able to gain inspiration and guidance on how to express her faith through fashion. This demonstrates the potential of the internet to not only provide religious knowledge but also to foster a sense of community and inspire self-expression among women.

These narratives emphasize the empowerment and agency that the internet can provide to Muslim women in their personal journeys of understanding and practicing their faith. By offering alternative perspectives, facilitating discussions, and providing access to diverse sources of information, the internet expands the opportunities for women to explore and engage with Islam in ways that resonate with their individual needs and experiences.

Further, a number of internet users explained that sometimes following a religious page helped them understand Islam. It was not always a mufti sharing a video; it could be something as simple as a quote image by a Muslim friend with a saying from Prophet Muhammad. Arifa explained this in her interview,

> Let's say, for me personally, if someone posts a quote or advice, maybe said by the Prophet or one of his companions, it is really nice to just get you through the day. It will be nice to remind you of that sort of thing.

The appeal of following online Sheikhs lies in the convenience and accessibility they offer. Young Muslims can engage with their teachings and guidance from the comfort of their own homes at any time that suits them. This accessibility allows them to incorporate religious learning and guidance into their daily lives, aligning with their digital-centric lifestyles.

However, it is important to approach the phenomenon of online Sheikhs with a critical lens. While many of these online scholars provide valuable insights and guidance, there is also a need for discernment and careful evaluation. The credibility, qualifications, and adherence to authentic Islamic teachings of these online figures should be considered, as the internet is not immune to misinformation or individuals with dubious intentions.

In conclusion, the trend of following online muftis and scholars among young Muslims has gained widespread popularity. These digital Sheikhs, with their large social media followings and relatable approach, have become influential voices in shaping the religious perspectives and knowledge-seeking behaviour of young Muslims. However, it is essential for individuals to exercise critical thinking, verify the credibility of these online figures, and seek guidance from established and qualified sources of Islamic knowledge to ensure a well-rounded understanding of their faith.

6.4 Weary of Authenticity

The acknowledgment of the need for caution and critical evaluation of online sources reflects the participants' awareness of the potential risks and limitations associated with relying solely on the internet for religious knowledge. While the internet offers a vast array of information, not all sources can be considered reliable or authentic.

Participants expressed various strategies to ensure the authenticity of the online sources they encountered. Authenticating information with imams or scholars emerged as a common practice, indicating the continued value placed on the guidance and expertise of traditional religious authorities. Seeking validation from trusted imams helps individuals navigate the vast amount of information available online and ensures they are adhering to accurate and reliable teachings.

Using trusted websites was another approach mentioned by participants. This implies the recognition of reputable online platforms known for providing reliable and authentic Islamic information. By relying on such websites, individuals can minimize the risk of encountering misinformation or dubious content.

Furthermore, the use of common sense as a tool to detect fallacies is an important aspect of critically evaluating online sources. Participants recognized the need to approach information with a discerning mindset, applying their own rationality and knowledge to distinguish between credible and questionable content. This highlights the importance of developing critical thinking skills when engaging with online sources.

Sumayya, who identified as Australian, aired her concerns over online websites and also presented a solution she had in place to authenticate information off the internet,

> I have [consulted the internet], but it is a very tricky area because you don't know what to trust on the internet. Anyone can write anything on the internet at this day and age, so I will do my research, but I will be cautious with what I am reading.

Haleemah tried to avoid the internet and preferred her parents' better guidance. She had not been able to find a way to trust the information relating to Islam on the internet completely. She said,

> Yeah, like, mainly I would go to my parents and ask them. They know more about it, and I would trust them more than the internet.

Eileen also shared a self-devised method of authenticating information off the internet. For her, if the answer was on a few websites, it was considered correct. She explained her method as,

> Google is a really good source because you have got a couple of sources claiming the same thing, and if they are a reliable thing, I do.

Similarly, in the US, Muntazir felt that while the internet was a questionable source for correct information, it did offer him a variety of perspectives.

He justified his use, despite the critique, saying it offered more varied views compared to an imam's singular view of a subject. He said,

> I don't have a go-to website that I do that. I typically just try to go online to different sources and try to understand each viewpoint and try to get something reputable, hopefully. It tends to be a little bit easier to do here and try to clarify or at least understand from both points of view.

Tasneem felt the same way but related to knowledgeable and elderly members of her family and friends circle to authenticate information. She said,

> I usually read on the internet to get different views, or I either ask a friend, like, if they know or, like, even ask an elder that knows religion.

For Noor, in addition to going to imams directly, the internet was a great source of information. She explained that she only followed pages or groups she considered authentic. They were described as authentic because they were run by a legitimate religious organization or a mufti she followed. She felt that answers to her questions on web forums of these platforms were answered by religious scholars as opposed to random people on the internet,

> There are websites where you can question. There are answers that do come from legitimate sources, and I do seek answers from those websites for some questions.

For Zia as well, there were certain sites that he felt were reliable. Apart from the vetted cites, his view of Google searches showcases his distrust in the platform for Islamic information. He explained,

> I only start from online, from websites that I know personally. However, I think that's very dangerous. Most people don't know a damn thing about where they're looking or what they're looking for. So, they start to take whatever Google spits out at the top and assume that that's the end result. I come with an understanding of how Google works and our technology magic. I know what the results show on the first, second pages. So, it's important for people to understand that they don't use all mediums to get a baseline understanding of what their response may or may not be.

For Yasir as well, the internet was a convenient tool as a "starting point," but beyond that, he would use imams or other knowledgeable persons for authentication,

> I try not to take the websites as truth because I don't know how to verify the people who are writing them myself. But I hate sites. If you have

> them in mind, if you have some names in mind, there's just one particular I like. I'll go to YouTube, listening to scholars, because then I can verify who's talking. But then let me see if I can find it. Islam Q&A. But even then, I won't use it. It's like a hard rule of thumb. Like, I got my ruling from this website. I'll use it to give me a little direction, the kind of questions I might ask about these topics, or things that come up. I use that as a starting point.

The use of the internet as a "starting point" was more common amongst male participants. In most cases, they had very easy access to imams and mosques to discuss the online results. Riaz, who lives in the US, shared his process of using the internet and the information's authentication by his community's imam,

> I think that is the first thing I do before I ask anyone – I search it online. I go online. If it is something, like anything in the holy Quran with a commentary that I can understand, that could, you know, answer the question, you know, that is the first thing that I go to. And if there is reliable hadith. I believe [you can] search online, search whatever the Quran says, or if there is a hadith on that, I would go towards that, and if there is clarification I need, if it is, like, really obvious to me, then okay, but if there is need of clarification, I would go to an imam.

Similarly, in the UK, Salman shared how he could just text his imam to authenticate the message. The idea of "just having a chat," "hanging out," or even "texting" an imam were not words or adjectives used by female participants. Salman's comments showcase this male privilege,

> Yeah, I mean initially, it is the first thing – that you check online. But what I like to do is message the imams themselves to get a better idea. So, I do that.

In a similar vein, Zeeshan also showcased how men have easier and wider access to mosques and, by default, the imam (who are men themselves). He explained,

> I'll usually try and gather as many sources of information as I can. But the first thing that I'd do would be the internet. And I'd gather as many internet sources as I can, then I would go to my community, and I'd turn to all the teachers at mosques who I keep in contact with. And I'll also turn to my parents as well. So, I'll have at least one or two resources. From my friends, family, community, but my most reliable resource is the internet and the teachers at my mosque.

Very few went to lengths similar to Sohrab. The young American devised a detailed mechanism to authenticate information by learning Arabic and its interpretation. He shared his measure with us,

> [What] I do is that, if I'm kind of confused about something in the Quran, I use the Quran Corpus Web site . . . and it's more of an academic source since I did study Middle Eastern and Islamic studies. I'm kind of not really afraid to engage with it in a more academic sense. So, it looks out, for example, the root of the Arabic word. Then I'll compare the usages to see kind of what you know, versus getting at. And then I'll try my best to apply it in that sense. I might look up different opinions that other people have had, but I don't take them at face value.

On the other hand, people like Latifah find it hard to trust the internet. She admitted trying to authenticate information from various sources but felt that nothing on the internet concerning faith-related matters could be taken too seriously. She narrated her opinion as follows,

> I would [use Google], but I wouldn't trust 100%. I would research, but I wouldn't trust 100%. It is hard to trust the internet.

Bashir also had a firm distrust of the internet as a source of fatwas. In his view, the lack of authentication was troubling. He explained his point as follows,

> Fatwas literally means a decree. And nowadays, anyone releases decrees. This is, like, the people that are not lawyers . . . that have no training in law. Issuing ethics about particular things, legal things. . . . They basically destroy all the traditional chain of knowledge that ensured that the people that talked about Islamic law, that they had permission, they had the training, and things like that. And I mean, there is a long story, but nowadays, you have people, somebody goes online to go out on a three-week training, and they come up with fatwas. I mean, it is unthinkable.

A few, such as Kinza, from the US, admitted there was no real way to authenticate information off the internet, yet she admitted that due to convenience, she kept using different sites. She elaborated,

> I usually just Google it and look at multiple websites that come up. I believe there's one called Islam Q&A, which, I think, anyone can answer questions on it. So, I know it's not the most reliable, but I have looked at that. And at Wikipedia as well.

Furthermore, some were worried about the negative impressions unauthentic fatwas might leave for both non-Muslims and Muslims. Nadia, from the US, was highly skeptical of online fatwas. During her interview, she shared this reservation,

> Who knows who randomly wrote [on online websites], and people are going to think it is true just because it is supposedly Islam Q&A and whatever, and people could have doubts about their own religion just because somebody so and so and Mr. Nobody decided to write something . . . as if they have the authority to say it is true and it is not, and people are going to automatically think it is without questioning it or looking into it further. I think that is, like, a really big problem with the internet. I mean, there are people in real life – I have heard all sorts of crazy satires from mosques and stuff – but I think on the internet, especially, there is like an extra set of 1,000 doors open to all sorts of misinformation and stuff that can really be harmful.

While most people in the interviews admired e-imams or influencer-imams, a handful were critical of them. Fizza, from the UK, felt that their popularity did not mean they were actual imams or well-educated to be informing thousands of followers. She explained her point of view,

> So, I follow some influencers not because I like them but out of interest, and they can say absolutely horrible things about people, like Shia minority, and about women, and there are Sheikhs that have hundreds and thousands of people following them, and have legitimacy they have in the community because of how many people are following them and for the people who are following them. They see how many people are following them and the way they dress, and they say, "Oh, wow, this must be correct!" and you can get led down the wrong path.

The presence of differing opinions and criticisms regarding e-imams or influencer-imams among the interview participants indicates a diversity of perspectives within the young Muslim community. While many individuals admired and appreciated the contributions of e-imams or influencer-imams, a minority expressed scepticism or criticism towards them.

The reasons for such criticisms can vary. Some participants might have raised concerns about the qualifications and credentials of e-imams or influencer-imams, questioning whether they possess the necessary religious knowledge and training to provide authoritative guidance. Others may have been sceptical about the authenticity and sincerity of these individuals, considering the potential for self-promotion or personal gain in the online realm.

Critiques of e-imams or influencer-imams may also arise from differing theological or ideological perspectives. Some individuals may hold more conservative or traditional views and perceive the content produced by these online figures as deviating from orthodox teachings. They might emphasize the importance of following established religious authorities and scholars who have received formal education in Islamic sciences.

It is essential to recognize that the rise of e-imams or influencer-imams is a relatively recent phenomenon, and the traditional role of religious authorities continues to hold significance in Muslim communities. The presence of criticism reflects a healthy scepticism and a reminder for individuals to exercise discernment when engaging with online sources of religious knowledge.

Overall, the diversity of opinions regarding e-imams or influencer-imams underscores the complexity of navigating the digital landscape and highlights the ongoing discourse within the Muslim community about the role and authenticity of online religious influencers.

6.5 Internet Use and Being "Good Muslims"

It is indeed intriguing that many participants in the interviews perceived their experience as Muslim users of social media to be distinct and unique. Their discussions shed light on various aspects of how they engaged with social media as a means to showcase the positive aspects of Islam, defend and justify their faith, engage in inter-faith dialogues, and utilize it as a tool for learning about Islam.

The recurring use of words such as "knowledge," "intention," "information," and "learn" in relation to the "good" use of social media by Muslims emphasizes the significance placed on acquiring knowledge about Islam and its various aspects, including elements of Sharia. For these young Muslims, social media serves as a platform to gain insights into their faith and share their knowledge and perspectives on Islamic matters.

Moreover, the word frequency analysis of the themes related to the "good aspects of social media" reveals the prevalence of words and their synonyms, such as "influence," "information," "powerful," "global," "show," "issues," "posts," "beliefs," and "Muslims." The frequent use of these terms suggests that young Muslims perceive social media as a powerful and global platform where they can share their beliefs, engage in discussions about various issues, and present Islam to a wider audience.

The following quotes from the participants further elucidate the intricate relationships and dynamics between young Muslims and social media, providing deeper insights into their motivations and experiences. These quotes help in understanding the significance of social media as a space for knowledge sharing, expression, and engagement with Islam on a global scale.

The interviews highlighted an important aspect: The internet not only provides a platform for Muslims to explore and engage with Islam but also allows non-Muslims to access and understand the religion in a way that challenges the biases they may encounter in mainstream media and society. For many participants, social media and online platforms served as a means to present a "good" or "true" representation of Islam, countering what they perceived as a biased portrayal of the religion in the media and society at large.

By utilizing the internet, young Muslims could directly share their perspectives, beliefs, and experiences, offering an alternative narrative to the prevailing stereotypes and misconceptions about Islam. This engagement with non-Muslims through social media platforms enabled them to bridge gaps in understanding and promote a more nuanced and accurate understanding of the religion.

In this context, the internet played a transformative role, empowering young Muslims to shape the narrative surrounding Islam actively and counter negative perceptions. By sharing their knowledge, experiences, and personal stories, they aimed to challenge stereotypes and contribute to a more inclusive and informed dialogue about Islam.

The internet, therefore, served as a space not only for Muslims to explore and express their faith but also as a platform for interfaith dialogue and understanding, where individuals from different backgrounds could engage in conversations and gain a more comprehensive understanding of Islam beyond biased portrayals in mainstream media.

Ameer also felt that humans can be biased, and the varied perspectives on the internet made it easy for people to detect this bias. He explained how both Muslims and non-Muslims could use the internet to get the right information about Islam,

> It is definitely better than bad because, especially for someone that wants to learn about Islam, it is such a big thing, because they can go online and have a biased opinion on their back, so they can just go and search for themselves, and even for Muslims who want to learn more it is there, it is definitely beneficial.

Jamilah further added to this perspective. She noted how positive or "hip" images of Muslims in online spaces were quite meaningful for the representation of Muslims. She elaborated,

> But it is good . . . I have seen more videos of Muslim people that people find funny and videos on Instagram where there are women in hijabs in it. I think that is a good thing because it shows how [our] people, we can laugh, and you know.

For Zubaida, in the UK, it was an opportunity to "reclaim" the image of Islam and Muslims. She explained,

> Social media is actually an informal view to cycling news, so when we see mainstream media to be problematic for Muslims and the portrayal and then you would instantly see Twitter, I would not say fight back, or just Muslims reclaiming their narrative through social media, this is the only means they have, it is accessible, and it is widespread, so I think it is a very much a powerful tool, and it would work in the favour of Muslims.

Zahid, who lived in Australia, said something quite similar to his counterparts in the UK. He talked about this "activism" and "correcting" the image of Muslims in the following manner,

> It allows a lot of people to stay in touch and know what is going on in each area, so, you know, you can't really hide acts of oppression and stuff as you are spreading awareness. So, if some Muslims feel that there is a lack of inclusivity, they can educate actually through social media and try and, you know, humanize Muslims more.

It was interesting to note that sectarian differences emerged in this regard as well. Liaqat, who shared his narrative, told us that his use of the internet also meant him spending time to "defend" and "clarify" misinformation about the Ahmadiyya community specifically. This meant that for non-Sunni groups, especially the marginalized ones, the "correct" information and "good image" issues were in relation to both non-Muslims and Muslims outside of their sect. Young Liaqat shared,

> I did like go on Twitter to, like, clarify any allegations against Islam and, like, my sect of Islam, Ahmadiyya.

The emergence of sectarian differences in the participants' experiences with the internet and social media further highlights the complex dynamics at play. In the case of Liaqat, his use of the internet was not solely focussed on exploring and clarifying his own understanding of Islam but also involved a sense of responsibility to defend and clarify misinformation about the Ahmadiyya community, which belongs to a marginalized sect within Islam.

For minority or marginalized Muslim groups, such as the Ahmadiyya community, the issue of presenting a "correct" and positive image of their sect became crucial not only for non-Muslims but also for other Muslims who may hold different beliefs or harbor misconceptions about their sect. The internet provided a means for them to address and counter these misconceptions, as well as to engage in inter-sect dialogue.

In this context, the internet served as a powerful tool for the Ahmadiyya community and other marginalized Muslim groups to reclaim their narrative, challenge stereotypes, and disseminate accurate information about their beliefs and practices. By utilizing social media platforms, they were able to directly engage with a wider audience and foster a more inclusive understanding of their sect within the larger Muslim community.

The experiences shared by Liaqat and others reflect the multifaceted nature of the internet's influence on sectarian dynamics within the Muslim community. While it offered opportunities for marginalized groups to amplify their voices and counter misinformation, it also exposed the existence of sectarian tensions and the need to actively engage in dialogue and bridge gaps between different sects for a more inclusive and informed discourse on Islam.

6.6 Conclusion

While participants in the interviews acknowledged the usefulness of the internet, they also demonstrated a critical approach towards the information they accessed. Many participants mentioned their efforts to authenticate the information they found online by utilizing other sources such as trusted websites, videos of reputable e-imams, or seeking confirmation from real-life imams or knowledgeable individuals. This indicates that young Muslims are actively engaged in a process of verification and cross-referencing to ensure the reliability and accuracy of the information they obtain.

The concept of "do it yourself Islam" (DIY Islam), as discussed by Whyte (2022), highlights the empowerment and agency that young Muslims experience through their engagement with online platforms. This notion resonates with the findings of this research, which demonstrate how young Muslims are able to navigate and sift through the information available on the internet to shape their understanding of Islam.

One important aspect that emerged from the interviews was the impact of cyberspace in breaking down gender barriers when it comes to accessing religious information. Traditionally, women seeking religious guidance or contacting an imam might have faced obstacles or cultural barriers. However, with the emergence of cyberspace, these gender barriers seem less prominent. Participants in the interviews shared their experiences of using online platforms to explore Islam and seek answers to their questions, regardless of their gender. This indicates that the internet provides a more accessible and inclusive space for women to engage with religious matters and overcome the challenges they may face offline.

By providing a platform where individuals can access information directly and bypass traditional gatekeepers, the internet has enabled young Muslims, including women, to take charge of their own religious journeys and seek answers to their questions independently. This shift towards a more inclusive and gender-neutral space in cyberspace contributes to the broader trend of empowering individuals and facilitating a greater sense of agency in their engagement with religious knowledge and practices.

The present study, in alignment with Eitzen (2019), contributes to the growing body of research indicating the emergence of new avenues for religious ideas. Notably, this study uncovers a distinct interest among participants in televangelist-style e-imams, who are perceived by young Muslims as progressive figures that reflect their lived experiences, employing familiar languages and tones and addressing relevant topics. The utilization of engaging multimedia formats, including reels, videos, and images, further enhances the appeal and accessibility of these e-imams as an ideal source of information. Consequently, this preference mitigates concerns about unauthenticated content from arbitrary websites. Overall, akin to previous literature, it is evident that the internet serves as a valuable tool for Muslims residing in Western societies to access religious information (Ahmed & Matthes, 2017; Brown,

2011; Safi, 2005). Nevertheless, the specific methods employed to seek such information and the extent to which it is relied upon vary among individuals.

A minority of Muslim participants in the interviews demonstrated a lack of concern regarding the authentication of information and were not proactive in seeking alternative means of verification. Their rationale for this approach was that they perceived the matters in question as trivial and not posing a threat to their faith. In some instances, participants attributed their lack of effort to verify information to laziness or a lack of motivation to explore other avenues for validation. This finding highlights the diversity of attitudes and behaviours among young Muslims in relation to the authentication of online information, indicating that not all individuals prioritize or engage in rigorous verification processes.

This chapter highlights the multifaceted role of cyberspace for Muslim youth, extending beyond information-seeking to providing a platform for self-expression. A significant theme that emerged was the participants' desire to use social media as a means to counter negative perceptions of Islam and Muslims, particularly in the post-9/11 environment. The mainstream media was seen as stigmatizing and lacking a fair representation of Muslims, leading many participants to feel compelled to showcase their "best selves" and address misconceptions about their faith in the informal yet influential online space.

An interesting aspect of our research is the inclusion of interviews with sub-sects, such as Ahmadiyyas, who face persecution from both mainstream society and within the broader Muslim community due to their distinctive beliefs. For this marginalized group, the online platform becomes a crucial tool to present their sub-sect in a positive light and counter both Islamophobia and sectarianism. By leveraging the power of social media, Ahmadiyyas seek to challenge negative narratives and assert their identity on online platforms.

The intersectional dynamics of Islamophobia and sectarianism further highlight the significance of the online space as a battleground for representation, where marginalized groups within the Muslim community can assert their agency and counter discriminatory narratives. This dimension of our research sheds light on the complexities of online engagement and how cyberspace can serve as a tool for resistance and empowerment for sub-sects facing multiple forms of discrimination.

Another curious subtheme of this section highlights the belief among many young Muslims that social media can be utilized for "good," particularly in terms of seeking Islamic information and guidance. This aligns with a study conducted by Frank van Tubergen and his team (2021) on practicing Muslims in the Netherlands, which found that a majority of participants frequently engaged with and followed Islamic pages and content on various social media platforms such as X, Facebook, and YouTube. Although the study did not examine the specific content, it focussed on tracking the participants' "likes" of religious content. Taken together, these findings suggest a consistent and ongoing reliance on social media platforms for acquiring formal Islamic knowledge, seeking moral guidance, and engaging with various aspects of religious practice. This highlights the significance of social media as a space where young Muslims can access religious information, connect with like-minded individuals, and engage in discussions related to their faith.

References

Ahmed, L., & Matthes, B. 2017. Religious authority in contemporary Islamic thought: The views of Tariq Ramadan. *Journal of Islamic Thought and Civilization*, 7(1), 1–16.

Amin, H. 2019. British Muslims navigating between individualism and traditional authority. *Religions*, 10(6), 354.

Berger, P. L., & Morgan, D. 2015. The role of religious leaders in public life. In *The role of religion in American politics* (pp. 163–182). Routledge.

Brown, J. A. 2011. Islamic reformulations: Belief, practice, and piety. In *Islam and society: Critical concepts in sociology* (pp. 207–238). Routledge.

Evolvi, Giulia. 2021. “Religion, New Media, and Digital Culture.” *Oxford Research Encyclopedia of Religion*. 23 Feb. 2021. https://oxfordre.com/religion/view/10.1093/acrefore/9780199340378.001.0001/acrefore-9780199340378-e-917

Magraoui, F. E., & Bouziane, M. 2017. The challenges of religious authority in contemporary Islam. *Journal of Muslim Minority Affairs*, 37(2), 235–249.

Nurdin, N. 2017. To research online or not to research online: using internet-based research in Islamic Studies context. *Indonesian Journal of Islam and Muslim Societies*, 7(1), 31–54.

Safi, L. 2005. The Public Role of the Ulama in Contemporary Islam: Out of the Garden. *The Muslim World*, 95(3), 427–448. https://doi.org/10.1111/j.1478-1913.2005.00112.x

Sisler, V. 2011. Cyber counsellors: Online fatwas, arbitration tribunals and the construction of Muslim identity in the UK. *Information, Communication & Society*, 14(8), 1136–1159.

van Tubergen, F., Cinjee, T., Menshikova, A., & Veldkamp, J. 2021. Online activity of mosques and Muslims in the Netherlands: A study of Facebook, Instagram, YouTube, and Twitter. *Plos One*, 16(7), e0254881.

Weimann, G. 2011. Cyber-fatwas and terrorism. *Studies in Conflict & Terrorism*, 34(10), 765–781.

Whyte, S. 2024. *Islamic religious authority in a modern age*. Palgrave Macmillan.

Whyte, S. A. 2022. Islamic religious authority in cyberspace: A qualitative study of Muslim religious actors in Australia. *Religions*, 13(1), 69.

Yilmaz, I. 2019. Potential impact of the AKP’s unofficial political Islamic law on the radicalisation of the Turkish Muslim youth in the west. In F. Mansouri & Z. Keskin (eds) *Contesting the theological foundations of Islamism and violent extremism. Middle East today* (pp. 163–184). Palgrave Macmillan.

7 Sharia and Civic and Political Participation

7.1 Introduction

The events of 9/11 have had a significant impact on the definition of a "good multicultural society" in many Western countries, leading to a heightened sense of Islamophobia and the need for Muslims to demonstrate their worthiness and counter negative perceptions. Understanding how young Muslims perceive the influence of their identity, personal belief systems, and the linkages between their faith and civic activities is essential, particularly considering the climate they have grown up in.

In this chapter, the concept of "acting citizenship" introduced by Isin and Nielsen (2008) is employed to explore the various acts of citizenship performed by young Muslims. The focus is on understanding the extent to which these acts are influenced by Sharia, the Islamic legal framework. By examining the relationship between faith and civic participation, the chapter aims to shed light on how young Muslims navigate their engagement in society based on their personal beliefs and identity. By delving into these aspects, the chapter aims to provide insights into the complex dynamics between faith, identity, and civic participation among young Muslims, considering the impact of the post-9/11 social and political climate.

Active participation within Muslim community organizations serves as a steppingstone for individuals to enrich their understanding of their role as active citizens. Local mosques, in particular, have evolved beyond their religious functions and have become multifunctional hubs that cater to the needs of newly migrated individuals and refugees. These mosques offer language courses, capacity-building workshops, leadership programs, outreach initiatives, and interfaith dialogue activities in addition to their religious services (Barton et al. 2013; Weller and Yilmaz 2012). Many of these activities are volunteer-driven, providing participants with tangible ways to take part actively in civic activities. By addressing issues such as migration, unemployment, social security, and multiculturalism, these community organizations raise awareness about socio-political issues, thus encouraging voting behaviour and fostering engagement in local politics.

DOI: 10.4324/9781003482604-7

The studies mentioned provide substantial evidence to support the idea that Muslim participation in civic and political activities extends beyond their own communities and is positively influenced by religious institutions such as mosques. Jamal (2005) found that Arab Muslims in New York who were associated with religious groups were more politically active, civically engaged, and had a stronger sense of group consciousness. Similarly, research by Bagby (2009, 2012) conducted among mosque-goers in the United States revealed that imams played a crucial role in encouraging political and civic participation among their followers. This suggests that religious leaders within the Muslim community serve as a driving force in promoting engagement within local communities.

McAndrew and Voas (2014) discovered that British Muslims actively participated in both spiritual and community-driven activities through their local mosques and faith-based organizations. Fleischmann, Martinovic, and Böhm (2016) found that the involvement of Turkish and Moroccan Muslims in ethnic or religious communities in the Netherlands was positively correlated with their level of political trust. Additionally, Moutselos (2020) identified a clear correlation between mosque attendance among Muslims in Western Europe and their probability of voting, terming mosques as "schools of democracy." These findings highlight the universality of the correlation between religious participation, community engagement, and political and civic activities among Muslims living in Western countries. It challenges the notion of lower voting probability among minority groups and emphasizes the importance of religious institutions in fostering democratic participation and political trust among Muslim communities in the West.

This chapter explores the issues of acting citizenship by focussing on Sharia. The following showcases whether Sharia is or is not a factor is shaping acts of citizenship in all three participants and also offers insight into previously unexplored issues, such as deciding to run for office or deeper exploration of understanding imams' guidance on these issues.

7.2 Sharia-Driven Political Thinking and Voting

When examining the theme of voting among young Muslims, two distinct perspectives emerge. The first perspective belongs to the young Muslim Secularists who consider Islam or faith as a private matter that does not have a direct influence on their voting decisions. The second perspective belongs to the Legal Pluralists who believe that being a Muslim does impact their voting choices, either by influencing whom they vote for or by influencing their decision to vote or abstain from voting altogether. It is important to note that these distinctions are unrelated to the Legal Pluralists A and B and Muslim Secularists A and B discussed earlier (Yilmaz 2012, 2023a, 2023b).

The fluidity of these perspectives suggests that the views of the young interviewees are adaptable and can vary from issue to issue. Their attachment or detachment to faith-inspired behaviour appears flexible and subject to change depending on the specific issue at hand. This fluidity may stem from the interviewees' personalized understanding and application of Sharia or, in some cases, a lack of comprehensive understanding of the concept's application in certain fields.

Another noteworthy aspect regarding voting preferences is the difference observed among participants from Australia, the UK, and the US. In Australia, many participants mentioned voting primarily because it is compulsory or due to family influence, with few expressing strong or detailed political opinions. On the other hand, participants from the UK and the US engaged in more extensive discussions about voting and the reasons behind their choices for specific candidates.

These findings highlight the diverse perspectives and motivations that shape the voting behaviours of young Muslims in different countries. The influence of religion on voting decisions varies among individuals, and cultural and contextual factors also play a role in shaping their preferences and level of political engagement.

7.2.1 ***Muslim Secularists***

The Secularists among young Muslims approach voting as a secular process that is separate from their religious beliefs. For them, faith does not play a significant role in shaping their voting behaviours. Instead, their voting decisions are based on personal preferences and considerations, such as alignment with a particular political party or candidate or following the voting patterns established within their families.

Some Secularists may feel a strong connection to a specific political ideology or party, driven by their passion for the party's goals or principles. Others, however, may view voting as a mandatory civic duty imposed by the state without necessarily having a deep interest or personal attachment to the political process. In these cases, the influence of Islam or religious beliefs on their voting decisions is minimal or non-existent.

Overall, Secularists prioritize factors such as personal choice, party platforms, and family voting traditions over religious considerations when it comes to participating in the electoral process. Their voting behaviours are largely independent of their faith, highlighting their adherence to a secular approach to politics.

Ajmal, who lived in Australia, explained that for him, voting was more of a compulsion due to the Australian government's regulation making it compulsory to vote. He explained,

> It is compulsory in Australia abut also, like, at the moment, I don't have one specific party, but if there is one specific party that I want to win, I wouldn't vote for them, I would vote for someone that would rather win and probably be in power, just to, yeah.

For the Australian interviewees who expressed secular opinions about politics, the most common reason for voting was its compulsory nature. Most felt obliged to vote as they would face a fine for missing out on voting.

Some were quite clear that they voted for parties that matched their political ideology. Summaya, from Australia, shared,

> Yeah, for example, I would vote for a party that supports gay marriage although that is religiously not supported, they have other views, for example, that align with mine and simply because it does not align with my religious view.

Similarly, Majeed also felt that Islam did not shape his political views, as he shared,

> No, my religion does not come in when I am voting because when I vote, it is mainly because "How will this benefit Australia?" and if they are promising healthcare, they won't do it specifically for religions, so my religion has nothing to do with it.

Ameer further added that his political views changed over time. With each election cycle, given the relevance of issues, he would decide which party to vote for. The young Australian explained,

> People in Australia, so one year you might me Labour, one year you might be Liberal, and one year I might be with the Green, and it definitely changes, so I definitely read up on different parties before elections, for sure.

Tooba felt that, for her, the policy of the electoral candidate mattered the most. She explained what led her to choose one candidate over another in UK politics,

> No [Islam does not influence by vote], not necessarily, no, I think it is more political reasons, but certain, like, for example, Labour, I find their campaigns to be more helpful towards the less advantaged people, so that is probably one of the reasons.

Many participants from all three countries voted because they felt it made some change or it was a citizen's responsibility to vote. Aleema, from Australia, shared,

> Well, every vote counts; every vote needs to be heard. And if there is a survey, if there is a vote, if there is any kind of information that the government seeks from me so that it can make my experience of living here a lot better, and if it affects the whole outcome in the smallest way, I would like to contribute to that.

Kinza from the United States pondered the relevance of faith in terms of personal politics. She explained why she felt these two did not influence each other,

> I think that in terms of Islam, you can make that a personal judgement call based on what you think your faith thinks is right or voting or not voting. I don't think in Islam that you have to do one or the other.

Haya also echoed the sentiments shared by Kinza,

> I don't think it's [voting] against Islam to vote. And I don't think it's against Islam not to vote beings. And so, I think that's sort of a personal choice.

It was also clear that, for many, voting based on personal opinions was really just beginning. Many were now living away from their parents and were starting to form mature opinions about politics. This meant that, for the first time, many were now totally deciding to vote on their own. Yusuf shared how this transition was taking place for him,

> I don't really think about the vote much because my parents would tell me how to vote, so it did not give us the opportunity to look at our own things. That is what I feel when I am older. So, I just listen to them.

For many young Muslims, the act of voting based on personal opinions was a relatively new experience. As they transitioned into adulthood and moved away from their parents' influence, they began to develop their own independent perspectives on politics. This shift allowed them to exercise their agency and make voting decisions that aligned with their individual beliefs and values.

Living away from their parents provided these young Muslims with the freedom to explore different political ideologies, engage in discussions with peers, and educate themselves about various political issues. This newfound autonomy empowered them to form mature opinions about politics and take responsibility for their own voting choices.

By independently deciding how to vote, these young Muslims demonstrated their growing maturity and engagement with the political process. They were no longer solely relying on the preferences or voting habits of their parents but were actively shaping their own political identities and participating in the democratic process on their own terms.

7.2.2 Legal Pluralists

Aisha, who lives in Australia, noted that voting, for her, was not heavily influenced by faith. However, she did feel that, in spirit, Islam promotes voting and participation in the democratic processes of the country in which one lives. She explained her views,

> That in Islam would promote voting, so promote people being treated equally and all of that, so the values behind that, I make sure that the party that I chose are the same. So, I don't vote for parties that benefit one group of the population and not everyone else. I would vote for parties that would ensure that everyone is treated equally and or would ensure that people who are vulnerable attain access to things that they need.

For Safdar, who lives in the US, voting is a civil duty, but he felt that Islam instilled this civic sense in Muslims. For him, voting is a driver of change, and Muslims, by their faith, are urged to be advocates for positive change. He explained his opinion of the issue,

> I do also believe that Islamically, you are supposed to help make changes for people who cannot help themselves. So, I think a lot of the things that we vote on for the community, and I think that you are supposed to help your community and be involved in your community, and you are supposed to try to voice your opinion. It is an Islamic fundamental that is instilled in you, and that definitely comes from my Islamic belief that you are supposed to try to make a change and help your community.

For Fatimah, from Australia, voting for candidates focussed on the Muslim community is important. Being from a minority group, she felt that her religious identity influences her voting preferences. She shared her opinion in detail,

> I think by voting, by getting involved. By voting, it means that the politicians, when they get up to, like, encourage people to vote for them, they have considered Muslim issues because of the Muslim votes, which can be very high in certain areas, and if Muslims don't vote, politicians have no reasons to make things better for Muslims.

Muntazir from the US also explained a similar opinion,

> Even in my Islamic reasoning and Islamic view, I believe that you have to do things within your system that you're in, and you cannot go and try to riot in the situation and whatnot because that's not going to lead anywhere.

Similarly, Anas shared that, for him, religion did not shape his vote until a political party was overly aggressive towards Muslims. It was more of a matter of identity politics that led him to these decisions, he explained,

> I guess the only reason if I were to vote with Islamic reasons in mind would be if a party is very anti-Muslim. And I was trying to find the best candidate who would be the least bad for Muslims. So, in terms of that, but in terms of "does my religion have anything with it," no.

Akbar, in the UK, also shared a similar point of view. He explained that his various identities as a Muslim, his ethnicity, etc., made him consider potential candidate's outlooks toward religious and ethnic minorities,

> Yeah, of course, whatever campaign does the most for ethnic minorities or religious wise, that is the first thing I look for, to be honest. Whether they would help ministries, etc., that would be my religious motivation behind voting.

In addition to being a responsibility, many shared that voting as a Muslim meant fighting oppression. Arben, who lives in the US, explained this view in the following way,

> Islam does not preach compliancy, and it teaches being proactive and taking all the means that are necessary for change and institute justice and positive and . . . for sure that is a motivation.

Khalifa, from the US, also felt that, for him, in addition to a host of social-political issues, it was also important to keep in view how his vote was going to impact Muslims at home and overseas. For him, religion did shape his voting patterns, which he explained,

> What we vote for affects everyone, including Muslims within and outside of America. And so, in that sense, I'm not quoting any hadith, also known in the Quran. But I think it's a requirement or number of Muslims who can.

Like Khalifa's views, Yasir also felt that since the US's political decisions impact the world, it is the voter's responsibility to vote on moral grounds. For him, a lot of this morality stemmed from faith. He added,

> If I vote in a politician and I don't feel confident that this politician has moral integrity. The amount of damage you can do at the head of the most powerful nation in the world, economically, culturally, and militarily, I don't see the benefits that this person will bring out outweigh the harm that this person will bring.

Maya was quite clear that not voting is not "un-Islamic;" however, for her, Islam motivated Muslims to vote for change and justice. The young British citizen explained,

> I think, if anything, Islam encourages us to vote because it expresses your opinion. I think in not voting, you're not doing something that's non-Islamic, but I think in voting, you are practicing Islamic principles because you've been given this responsibility of contributing to something that you can make better.

Amongst participants from the UK and the US, there was a clear sense that Muslims need to vote for representation, or their lack of voting was a negative image for the community. For instance, Zia, a young American, shared,

> As Muslims, we have to do what's in the best interest of the community. . . . And voting does not conflict with our own with disputes. Voting is one of the only ways we can actually have a voice. And by sharing our opinions of others, we can get other people to vote the same way that we'd like for them to vote. That's how you end up having a voice. . . . It's our obligation to take part in society.

Aqil's statement further sheds light on this issue. He argued that he would like to see a Muslim politician in office or someone unbiased toward the community. He felt that around election season in Australia, at times, the debates stereotype and vilify Muslims. These factors, in his view, impact his voting and political outlook. He discussed,

> Islamic reason, it depends on that people before the election, all of them have speech and the people who are rude to Islam and that kind of stuff that makes you disappointed, "Oh, this person doesn't like Muslims."

From the UK, Shiza also felt that she felt pulled towards voting for candidates who wanted to uplift minorities. Referring to Jeremy Corbin, she explained her point of view,

> He was trying to do a lot, and he was part of the Labour Party, and he was trying to do a lot not just for the Muslim community but the minority itself, so that is why, based on why, a lot of people voted for him, and we were quite surprised when he did not win because a lot of people were rooting for him. I think he would have been so good for not only the Muslim community but for the overall minorities who are struggling in the overall British community.

Behlul felt that civic participation was something that was encouraged in Islam. For him, American politics was distasteful at times and had many issues, but he was quite clear that Islam encourages its followers to take part in society. He said,

> But it is a civic duty. It's something that's motivated in Islam being human.

Ashar's statement adds more detail to the idea,

> And you know, the Holy Prophet of Islam, a saying where he says that a love of nation is part of faith, so if you love your nation, of course, you are going to do everything in your power to make sure that it is on the right path, you could say, or it is moving towards the better side.

Saad extended this debate and felt it was problematic to have Muslims not voting in the UK. He explained this in the following way,

> I think many Muslims don't vote. So, if you don't vote, you can't really complain about anything. Yeah, of course, having Muslim candidates or candidates that are somewhat sympathetic to Muslim needs, you know, addressing the problems we face, particularly around racism and being treated differently. You know the abuse every now and then, it is a big thing.

No one felt religion stopped them from voting. Many showed awareness about this school of thought but mainly dismissed it as conservative or irrelevant to them. Fizza, from the UK, explained she was aware of this view but did not agree with them.

> I think there are some religious speakers that may push a notion that you should not get involved in British democracy because it is incompatible with Islam and things that you may indirectly be voting for, for example, maybe acceptance of LGBT communities, and they are making laws on depending on who you vote whether they are left or right and aren't seen or are not compatible with Islam, whether it is equality or gender.

Among participants, there was a distinct understanding of the importance of Muslim representation in the political arena. They recognized that voting played a crucial role in ensuring that the voices and interests of the Muslim community were heard and represented in the decision-making process. Therefore, there was a sense of responsibility and urgency to vote in order to have a say in shaping policies and addressing the needs of their community.

Furthermore, participants expressed concern that the lack of Muslim voter participation could perpetuate negative stereotypes and misconceptions about the Muslim community. They recognized that their collective absence from the voting process could contribute to a perception that Muslims were disengaged or apathetic towards civic duties, potentially undermining efforts to challenge Islamophobia and promote a positive image of Muslims in society. In this context, voting was seen as a means to actively contribute to the representation and visibility of Muslims in the political landscape. By participating in the electoral process, they believed they could counteract negative narratives, promote inclusivity, and work towards the betterment of their community.

7.3 Consulting Imams on Political Issues

In this study, we encounter a notable distinction between two groups of participants: The legal pluralists and the secularists. However, it is crucial to emphasize that these categories should not be conflated with the "pluralist" and "secularist" classifications discussed in Chapter 4. Instead, within the context of this section, the legal pluralists are characterized by their inclination to consult imams or religious sources when confronted with political issues. For some, this consultation takes the form of ongoing and regular conversations, serving as a consistent source of guidance and insight. In contrast, others may seek guidance from imams or religious sources on a more ad hoc basis, posing specific questions or seeking clarification on particular topics.

The legal pluralists' choice to consult imams or religious sources on political matters reflects their belief in the importance of incorporating Islamic teachings and principles into their decision-making processes. They view their faith as a comprehensive framework that extends beyond individual spirituality, encompassing various aspects of life, including politics. These individuals perceive their religious leaders as knowledgeable authorities who can provide valuable insights and interpretations of Islamic teachings in the context of contemporary political issues.

On the other hand, the secularists in this study maintain a distinct perspective, asserting that Islam or faith does not significantly influence their political participation or shape their political outlook. They prioritize a separation between religion and politics, viewing politics as a realm governed by secular principles, policies, and ideologies. For them, voting decisions and political engagement are primarily driven by personal opinions, ideologies, and pragmatic considerations rather than religious guidance.

It is worth noting that a range of views and degrees of influence exists within both groups. Some legal pluralists may adhere more strictly to the guidance provided by imams or religious sources, considering it a central factor in political decision-making. Others may take a more nuanced approach, considering religious guidance as one among several factors that inform their political perspectives. Similarly, among the secularists, some may completely disregard the influence of religion on politics, while others may acknowledge the broader ethical principles derived from their faith that can inform their political engagement without directly consulting religious authorities.

These findings underscore the complexity and diversity of perspectives within the Muslim community regarding the relationship between Islam and politics. The existence of legal pluralists and secularists reflects the multifaceted nature of individual beliefs and practices, highlighting that there is no monolithic approach among young Muslims in interpreting and applying Islamic teachings to political matters.

The participants in this study exhibited a diverse array of political questions that they sought to address through consultations with imams, both in person and online. These inquiries encompassed a wide range of international and national political issues that held significance for the participants and their communities.

On an international level, the participants sought guidance on topics such as the conflict in the Middle East, including the Israeli-Palestinian conflict and the war in Syria. They were interested in understanding the Islamic perspective on these conflicts and the role of Muslims in responding to and engaging with such crises. Additionally, questions were raised about the treatment of Muslims in various countries, including issues of discrimination, Islamophobia, and human rights abuses.

At the national level, participants sought guidance on political participation, voting, and civic engagement. They were interested in understanding the Islamic stance on participating in democratic processes, including whether it is permissible to vote and how to select candidates who align with Islamic values. Furthermore, discussions were held on social justice issues, including poverty, inequality, and the responsibility of Muslims to address these concerns through political action.

The participants also sought clarification on the compatibility of Islamic teachings with specific policies or laws in their respective countries. This included inquiries about gender equality, LGBTQ+ rights, freedom of speech, and religious freedom. They sought to navigate the intersection between their religious beliefs and the prevailing legal and political frameworks, seeking guidance on how to reconcile potential conflicts and make informed decisions.

The availability of online resources, such as videos featuring imams discussing political topics, provided an additional avenue for seeking guidance and clarification. Participants utilized these online platforms to access a wide range of perspectives and interpretations, expanding their understanding of Islamic teachings in relation to contemporary political issues.

The diversity of the questions posed to imams reflects the participants' desire to align their political engagement with their religious beliefs and principles. By seeking guidance from imams, they aimed to deepen their understanding of Islam's perspective on various political matters and navigate the complexities of engaging in political discourse and decision-making as Muslims.

Zakria shared that a political discussion was more of a one-time question he explored with this local imam. He explained,

> Yeah, the imam was Australian, but we weren't talking about Australian politics. Syria, I just wanted to get his point of view on what was going on.

Zeeshan, who had regular interactions with his local imam, had a wider range of political issues he discussed. He shared that current political and social issues were mostly discussed,

> I mean not only politics, but we've discussed recent news related to Covid, the UK's reaction to Covid. We just discussed how Boris Johnson and the MPs in the UK have reacted to it, and it doesn't make sense how the decisions are made. For example, most recently, we've got schemes where they're encouraging people to go to restaurants, followed by a crackdown [on eating out], within the space of a month

> or two. And it has created a lot of confusion. That would be my most recent discussion.

Sheeba, also from the UK, also explained how current political issues became her point of consultation. She used a religious scholar as opposed to a mosque imam to discuss political issues. She elaborated,

> It had to do with the Black Lives Matter movement. There was a trend on social media where a lot of Muslims were supporting the Black Lives Matter movement. They failed to understand that a lot of Black people are Muslims, but when Black Lives Matter became a big thing, a lot of people tried to cancel it by saying that we should be focussing on Yemen and Syria and other Muslim countries. But it really got to mean that a lot of Muslims don't see Black people as their own community. So, I reached out to a scholar to understand more about this matter and to raise awareness about it.

Indeed, the consultations with imams or scholars by the pluralist participants in this study served as a means to gain knowledge and understanding of the Islamic perspective on political issues. These consultations were not intended solely to rely on the imams' verdict or narrative but rather to inform the participants about the teachings and principles of Islam in relation to the specific political topics discussed.

By seeking guidance from imams, the pluralist participants aimed to expand their knowledge base and engage in informed decision-making. They recognized that Islamic teachings have a role to play in shaping their perspectives on political matters, and consulting imams allowed them to access the scholarly interpretation of these teachings.

However, it is important to note that the consultations with imams were not the sole source influencing the participants' opinions. The pluralist participants engaged in a broader process of information gathering, which included seeking multiple perspectives, conducting independent research, and engaging in discussions with peers and community members.

The consultations with imams provided a foundational understanding of the Islamic perspective, but the participants critically evaluated this information and integrated it with their own experiences, values, and knowledge. They recognized the need for a nuanced and contextual approach to political issues, considering various factors such as social, cultural, and historical contexts as well as individual circumstances.

In this way, the consultations with imams served as a starting point for the pluralist participants to develop their own informed opinions and perspectives on political issues. They recognized the importance of considering multiple viewpoints and engaging in critical thinking to navigate the complexities of politics in light of their Islamic faith.

Safdar's statement makes this very clear when he states,

> I would say that, yes, I have discussed political issues with imams and scholars in my community. They are usually based in Chicago, and all of these conversations that I have had are face-to-face. . . . So, there have been political issues like abortion, gay marriage, gun laws, and I have asked about organ donations, I have asked about marriage, and I have asked about just the overall political issue and current events and . . . war and what the Islamic perspective is on the issue, or if we are going into another country and there is a trade deal, so what is the Islamic perspective on that issue.

Amjad also shared a similar view. The young Australian explained that his visits to the imams were to gain more insight into current issues from an Islamic perspective. He added,

> Yes, I have discussed political issues, usually to do with foreign policy, Western foreign policy. And a lot of philosophical problems in the Muslim community I have also discussed with imams.

Liaqat, who lives in the US, also explained that while he had information about issues such as the murder of Gorge Floyd, he had been discussing this issue with an imam to understand the Islamic perspective on police brutality.

Sometimes, political themes were something mosque-goers came across without taking the initiative. Weekly Friday khutbahs (addresses) usually discuss political themes from a religious point of view. Raheel's experience showcases this indirect source of information,

> No, I have not personally discussed political issues with imams. I have definitely listened to imams talking about political issues; whether it is Friday prayer sermons, they could be talking about issues going on in Kashmir or the issues the Muslims are facing in Iran. When and where I have gone ahead to seek advice with an imam, it has basically been to theological purposes, not political.

Muntazir, from the US, explained that, for him, most of this knowledge about religion's take on political issues comes from lectures held at different institutes, local community centres, etc. He elaborated,

> Political issues, yeah, I mean, there have been people, scholars, mostly in lectures. It was never online. But there are a lot of sources now that you can go online. Lectures are by highly qualified people and one can go in and listen and learn about issues.

Sohrab's statements also indicate that lectures at think-tanks, community centres, mosques, etc., became a source of Islam's political outlook. While he did not agree with the source on the matter, he did share how it was a source of political thought for many Muslims in his community,

> Back when I was in college with this same imam that I mentioned earlier, he is actually having his own libertarian think tank. So, he really emphasizes, you know, libertarian things, which is kind of interesting because that's not the first thing people think that Muslims are. I don't necessarily agree with him politically, but in that sense, I might have come across some political discussions with him.

In contrast to the pluralist participants, a smaller but significant number of young Muslims from Australia, the UK, and the US expressed the belief that discussing political issues with imams or religious scholars was unnecessary or even irrelevant. For these participants, religion was viewed primarily as a spiritual and personal matter, separate from the realm of politics.

These individuals held the perspective that politics and governance were secular domains guided by laws, policies, and democratic processes rather than religious teachings. They did not see a direct connection between their faith and political engagement and thus did not find it necessary or beneficial to seek religious guidance on political matters.

For them, politics was seen as a practical and pragmatic realm that required them to consider the interests and welfare of society as a whole without the need for specific religious interpretations. They believed that their political opinions and decisions should be based on their own values, principles, and assessment of the issues at hand rather than relying on religious authorities.

Hakeem, from Australia, explained this view during his interview,

> I don't discuss political issues with Sheikhs for the most part because I just don't think they would have the most objective views on political issues.

Ebrar was also quite clear on this stance when he said,

> I think that scholars and religious people should not get involved with politics. They should be involved with their job. Their job is to spread the word of Islam, not the political party.

As opposed to Ebrar, Asher from the US explained how he felt Islam had political views, which he explored, but those did not lead him to form his political opinions. The young man explained,

> Of course, there are teachings of that in Islam, in how to base an economy and how to base a country and whatnot, but from a personal view, you have your own political views, and that does not dictate your religion and how you interpret your religion. Of course, religion should dictate your political views but not something that is making it.

It is important to note that the perspective of these participants does not imply a lack of religious commitment or a dismissal of the importance of faith in their lives. Instead, they viewed religion and politics as separate spheres, each with its own distinct role and influence. They preferred to navigate political issues through secular frameworks, such as human rights, social justice, or individual values, rather than seeking religious guidance.

This perspective highlights the diversity of attitudes among young Muslims regarding the intersection of religion and politics. While some participants emphasized the importance of consulting imams and scholars for religious insights on political matters, others saw religion as detached from the political realm. Both perspectives reflect individual interpretations and understandings of the relationship between faith and politics, influenced by personal beliefs, experiences, and social contexts.

7.4 Running for Office

The exploration of political views among the participants also looked at their perceptions of whether Islam encouraged or discouraged Muslims from running for political office. This line of inquiry resulted in the emergence of two distinct themes, reflecting differing perspectives among the participants.

The first theme highlights the views of those who believe that Islam either prohibits or encourages Muslims to participate in politics and seek political office. Within this group, there were varying interpretations of Islamic teachings and principles regarding political engagement. Some participants felt that Islam discourages active involvement in politics, perceiving it as a worldly and potentially corrupting sphere. They believed that the focus of a Muslim's life should primarily be on religious obligations and spiritual matters rather than engaging in the complexities and compromises of political life.

On the other hand, there were participants who held the belief that Islam actually encourages Muslims to be actively involved in politics and to seek political office. They saw politics as a means to contribute to society, advocate for social justice, and promote the interests of their community. These individuals believed that Muslim representation in political institutions was crucial for addressing the concerns and needs of the Muslim population and other marginalized communities. They saw no inherent contradiction between being a practicing Muslim and being involved in politics, viewing political participation as a way to influence society positively and uphold Islamic values.

The second theme that emerged was the perspective of secular participants who did not perceive a direct link between Islam and the decision to run for political office. For them, the decision to engage in politics was based on personal interests, beliefs, and a sense of civic responsibility rather than being influenced by religious considerations. They viewed political participation as a matter of individual choice and saw no inherent requirement or barrier imposed by their faith.

Tasneem from Australia shared her view on the issue. She explained,

> Well, Muslims are a population of Australia, so obviously politicians and all that they have to reflect the community. Well, obviously, they can give their views like any other citizen or Australian.

Zulaikha, who lives in the UK, noted that there are many opportunists for Muslims to enter politics. She said,

> I mean [Muslims] can become the Mayor of London, for example, like Siddique.

In a similar fashion, Rizwan also shared similar excitement and sentiments on the matter,

> Yeah, of course! You have got Saqqaq Khan, who has become the Mayor of London, and then you have got Sajid Javed, who has become an MP, and he was the Foreign Sectary at one stage, so I think there was a Chancellor, yeah, definitely, I think, because Islam encourages you to make a difference in the country that you are in.

Khalifah, who lives in the US, also felt that not only did faith allow political participation, it was essential to represent the interests of Muslims. He explained,

> They can bring a diversity of ideas. Representation, having a Muslim voice. And also changing the perception of Muslims treat people who have a negative perception of Muslims.

Muntazir even went as far as to suggest that, as Muslims, it is important to bring change to things rather than complain. He felt that the only way to bring change to corrupt systems was to run for office. He explained,

> So, I think it's necessary for all Muslims who are interested in changing something about the policy, the politics especially they have.

Ajola from the US also felt that seeing more Muslims involved in US politics was something she cherished and hoped to see continue. She noted,

> I think that now you see more Muslim candidates and Muslims being more involved in politics and in public service, and I think that's great because, for a long time, the Muslim voices were not heard. And now people are getting more involved.

Some participants expressed the belief that having Muslim representatives in political offices not only had an impact on the Muslim community within their respective countries but also had broader implications for Muslims worldwide. They saw Muslim political leaders as potential advocates who could address issues and challenges faced by Muslims both domestically and internationally.

These participants believed that Muslim political representatives had the potential to influence policies and decisions that directly affected the lives of Muslims, such as issues related to religious freedom, discrimination, and social inclusion. They felt that having Muslim voices in positions of power could bring about greater understanding and representation of Muslim perspectives, leading to more inclusive policies and a better recognition of the rights and needs of Muslim communities.

Furthermore, they believed that the presence of Muslim representatives in political offices could challenge negative stereotypes and combat Islamophobia on a global scale. By demonstrating the achievements, capabilities, and contributions of Muslims, these representatives could help shape a more positive and nuanced narrative about Islam and Muslims, countering the prevailing prejudices and misconceptions that exist in many societies.

In this sense, the participants saw Muslim representation in politics as not only important for addressing local issues but also for exerting a positive influence on the perception of Muslims worldwide. They viewed it as an opportunity to challenge stereotypes, promote understanding, and foster greater respect and acceptance of Islam and Muslims in the global community.

Habiba shared her joy over seeing Muslims women in Congress and further added,

> I appreciate them because I think they most closely align with my views. I'm especially proud of them because they mentioned Palestine a lot, and they work on issues of Palestinian rights. And that's something that, for the longest time, has been so taboo. Like, you would just be blacklisted for even saying the word Palestine. And they're really bringing that view into the mainstream. And so, I think that's really important.

A significant number of participants expressed the belief that Western countries generally do not prevent politicians from practicing their religion. They did not see a fundamental conflict between being a practicing Muslim and holding a political office in Western democratic societies.

These participants emphasized the importance of religious freedom and the right of individuals to freely practice their faith, including those in positions of political power. They believed that Western countries, with their principles of pluralism, tolerance, and freedom of religion, generally respected the rights of individuals to adhere to their religious beliefs while engaging in political activities.

According to their perspective, Western democracies value diversity and inclusivity and do not impose restrictions or obstacles on politicians based on their religious affiliations. Instead, the focus is more on the qualifications, competence, and alignment with the values and interests of the constituency.

As long as politicians uphold the laws and principles of the country, they see no inherent barrier to Muslims practicing their religion while holding political office.

Hasan, from Australia, explained this point,

> If you become a politician in Australia, that means you have to follow the Australian law and, in a way, you can be a good Muslim and a politician at the same time. I think Australia does give you the freedom to follow your religion and be a politician at the same time. I think it will work out.

Similarly, Noriya saw faith as a personal matter which did not interfere with politics. In her view, Muslims should and could pursue politics,

> Because politics is not based on religion. Politics is based on, you know, how passionate you are about changing issues that people are facing, so not everything is about religion.

Even when the young respondents were unsure of Muslim politicians in their respective countries, they liked the idea of having representation in politics. Zakria noted that,

> I don't even know if there are influential Muslim politicians or ministers right now, but [we could] definitely work on that.

Indeed, for many respondents, the presence of Muslims in politics served as a source of encouragement and inspiration. Seeing fellow Muslims holding political office provided them with role models to look up to and aspire to if they were interested in a career in politics.

These respondents recognized the significance of representation and the importance of having individuals from their own community involved in the political decision-making process. They believed that Muslim politicians could bring a unique perspective and understanding of the experiences and challenges faced by Muslims, which could contribute to more inclusive and equitable policies.

The visibility of Muslim politicians also challenged stereotypes and misconceptions about Muslims in society. It helped to counter negative narratives and Islamophobia by showcasing the diversity, achievements, and contributions of Muslims in the political arena. By seeing Muslims successfully navigate the political landscape, these respondents felt encouraged and empowered to actively participate in politics and make a difference in their communities.

Having Muslim role models in politics also provided a sense of validation and belonging for these respondents. It reinforced the idea that Muslims can fully participate in all aspects of society, including politics, without compromising their religious identity or values.

Zia, who was passionate about US politics, noted this point,

> Voicing the fact that they are Muslim is a huge part because it empowers the next generation to know that if this person could be called mayor, that I could become a senator.

Hiranur further added that it is also a chance for Muslims to not only create role models but also eliminate biases and stereotypes regarding Muslims. She felt that the presence of Muslims in Congress was essential because,

> It also shows that because there are also perceptions of Muslims there, more will be educated. Like, some Muslims countries . . . they don't care about human rights or woman educational rights. They just care about early marriages and stuff like that. But when you see those things, of course, it changes the whole picture. But all of those, it can also be a good sign. Leading in the rights decision with their knowledge, with their performance, could make a difference.

Zohaib, who was a participant from the UK, noted a similar appeal of Muslim participation in politics. He explained how it gave a change to "clear the name" of Muslims,

> I think we can tell people about Islam; I think we can show white people that they are wrong a lot of times. I think we can make things better for us, and we can make things better for other people of colour, and we can go into the shoes of other people who have also suffered, who are suffering, and who have been discriminated against. But unfortunately, we also do not have that unity and British Muslim politicians, some of them I have spoken to, and I know politicians who are British across the political spectrum, some of them are good, generally speaking – they are just politicians.

Asifah, who lives in Australia, shared similar views,

> If they do a good job, if they gave it their best, it would give a really good name to the Muslim identity, if they are doing a good job in politics.

Aleem, also from Australia, called political participation a chance "*to show the [Australian community] what we are about.*" Imran used the abbreviation "PR" to explain how political patriotism will help Muslim Australians. He explained,

> We can try to represent ourselves better. We can show them that we are not after enacting Sharia law in their country like here they want to do. Muslim countries have the highest amount of charity compared to every

> other single country in the entire world. We have a lot of good to offer, and yeah, we aren't exactly expressing it that well. Representation is, I think, the main thing that we can do better in our PR relations.

While the majority of respondents did not see the idea of Muslim politicians as outrageous, there were indeed a few who expressed objections and raised concerns about political involvement. One particular objection that emerged was the fear of compromising Islamic principles and engaging in actions that may be perceived as immoral or conflicting with religious teachings.

Some respondents expressed reservations about politicians having to engage in activities such as lying, lobbying, and aligning with interests that may not align with their understanding of what is "purely Islamic." They were cautious about the potential ethical challenges and compromises that politicians may face in the political arena.

Among these objections, Hakeem from Australia held a more specific viewpoint regarding women who identify with Islam pursuing politics. He believed that women should not hold political office, although he did not provide a detailed explanation for this belief. His perspective seemed to stem from the notion that there are certain gender roles and expectations within Islam that may influence his perspective on women's involvement in politics.

Arben, who lives in the US, did not object to the idea of Muslims participating in politics but cautioned against the temptations of being corrupted by the system. He noted,

> I mean, as long as you stick to your Islamic principles, you can be a politician. I do not think trying to be a politician in America is against Islam; if anything, I think it is an approach to kind of rise to power your people and help your community. But at the same time, we need to be careful not to forsake our values and try to please others, but other than that, it is perfectly okay.

Affan, from the UK, felt quite pessimistic about Muslim politicians in the UK. He admitted that he saw Muslims in politics, but he was not sure whether it was a good thing or that it did not conflict with Islam. He shared an example to explain his views on the issue,

> Sajid Javed being in the Cabinet and being a Muslim, but even then, he was still protecting Boris Johnson, whereas I feel like . . . Boris Johnson is still racist. Yeah, I don't see it, and Islam is not going to have a powerful position in British culture and society. I don't think it is happening.

Tooba also felt that a "strong-minded" Muslim could participate in British politics, as there was a lot to tempt them to change course. She explained,

> I think if you are a very strong-minded individual, I think you can do it. But you can't be easily influenced, especially if it is in a Westernized

> country; you need to stand by your own cultural roots and your own religion, and if you want to make an impact, because sometimes you see there are some Muslim political leaders and they tend to be more modernized and their approach is quite moved away from religion, just to win more votes or trying to fit into society. So, I do think it can be done, but the individuals themselves have to be quite strong-minded.

Qaiser was not opposed to the idea of Muslims running for office, but he felt that modern politics always ended up in moral compromises. The "compromises" he explained conflicted with the morals taught by Islam. The young Britisher explained,

> There is not such law set in stone that makes it incompatible, but with Islamic ethics, modern politics requires compromise, modern politics requires you often to follow the lobby groups or the follow the money or to because susceptible to people and power, and other people in power, and that is where you could compromise with your faith.

Raheel, also from the UK, echoed a similar view of the issue,

> Because a lot of the fundamentals of British politics [are] against Islamic teaching, you know, where a lot of British politics includes simple things . . . like you cannot make some money and banks, etc. It is all based on tax and loans, etc., and that is something that is against Islam. . . . Even in Islamic countries, if you are a politician, you get corrupt. What I am saying is that some of the fundamentals of politics in the UK, they just go against Islamic teachings; you cannot really get involved in them.

The prevalence of concerns about compromising "Islamic morals" in the pursuit of political goals among participants from the UK suggests a variation in perspectives among the different countries included in the study. Participants from the UK were more likely to raise this issue than their counterparts from Australia and the US.

This divergence in views could be influenced by a range of factors, including cultural and religious contexts, as well as the specific experiences and backgrounds of the participants. Different regions and communities may have varying understandings and interpretations of Islamic ethics and the extent to which they should guide political engagement.

Overall, the participants' views on running for political office reflected a range of opinions regarding the role of Islam in political engagement. While some felt that Islam either discouraged or encouraged political involvement, others saw no direct link between their faith and the decision to seek political office. However, a common sentiment among many participants was the importance of minority representation and the need for diverse voices in political decision-making processes. They believed that having Muslims in positions of political power was essential for effective representation and advocating for the interests of their communities.

7.5 Sharia-Driven Thinking and Civic Participation

The participants' views on Islam's permissibility and its relationship with social and community work and protesting can be categorized into two main groups: those who hold a secular view and those who believe that Islam encourages such civic participation.

The secular-leaning participants see their involvement in social and community work, as well as participating in protests, as independent of their religious beliefs. They view these activities through a secular lens, driven by their personal values, sense of social responsibility, and the desire to bring about positive change in society. Their engagement in these activities is not specifically motivated by their spiritual belief system but rather by a more general sense of civic duty or a desire for social justice.

On the other hand, there is a group of participants who perceive Islam as encouraging and inspiring their involvement in social and community work, as well as protesting. For them, these activities are deeply rooted in their spiritual belief systems and are seen as acts of faith. They interpret Islamic teachings as promoting social justice, compassion, and the obligation to help others, which motivates their active engagement in various forms of civic participation. Their religious beliefs serve as a guiding force in their commitment to social activism and community service.

Haya, who lives in the US, noted that Islam, at its core, forces people to work towards improving themselves and their communities. So, any civic participation, for her, was linked to faith. She explained,

> Well, in Islam, it says if they believe it's in the Quran, you know, a law will not change people till they change themselves. I mean, as a Muslim, what people need to do is really start looking at some of the diseases in their own hearts, working on themselves, working on their families. And these circles go out and broader, broader. So, you get the community. We really need to change ourselves. And that's really practicing Islam the way it should be practiced. And there's a lot of leeway in that. And there's a lot of flexibility and there's a lot of room for different ways to practice it. But so, we really need to change ourselves and become better Muslims if we really want to change society.

Amjad, who lived in Australia, also shared that, for him, the spirit of service was a value instilled in him by his faith. He helped Muslim students on campus and was active in organizing and participating in inter-faith events to promote harmony.

In addition, faith as an identity also shaped civic engagement. For instance, identification with "Muslim causes" was a common motivation. Bihter, from the UK, shared an example,

> The physical protests that I went to, one was the Palestinian one that I had personally felt like, since I was young, going to an Islamic school, we always talked about "Muslims are being attacked around the world," and Palestine was always on top of our list, it was the most prominent, especially when I was younger there was a lot of focus on Palestine, so that was one of the pushes, like, also my family was going as well. It was like a family activity we did, we went to, and we protested, and the most recent one was the Syria protest I went to, also similar Muslims – this time it was Muslims killing Muslims, and it was atrocious, so I went out there, and I protested.

Ali, who aspired to be a politician, also hinted at this aspect of identity politics. The young Australian said,

> As Muslim politicians, the main agenda would be to combat Islamophobia and to educate people and help the poor and the needy. And ensure that the policies and laws they put in place are fair and just for everyone.

It was not uncommon to find online activism in the form of singing petitions for causes related to protesting the Rohingya genocide and the wars in Syria or Palestine. Taking part in student association activities and local mosque activities was also common among the participants. This was again a reflection of their identity as Muslims. Zia shared his motivations behind this participation,

> So, I've always been involved on a grassroots level, helping or engaging the local young Muslim audience into getting involved with the local communities one way or another.

Adding to this discussion, Safdar, also from the US, felt that this engagement aided in the "good image" creation of Muslims. The young participant explained,

> So, if I am working in my community and Muslims in every other community in the USA are working in their community, I think that can be huge! Because eventually, every community will start realizing that Muslims are not as fearful as they think. I think we can actually try to rectify some of the issues in minority communities by doing that work

Indeed, the motivations for civic engagement among young Muslims are multifaceted, and faith-related matters are not the sole factor driving their participation. Many participants also expressed a strong commitment to secular causes and engaged in charitable activities that were not explicitly tied to their religious beliefs.

These young individuals recognized the importance of addressing social issues and making a positive impact in their communities, irrespective of religious affiliations. They were driven by a sense of empathy, compassion, and a desire to contribute to the well-being of others, regardless of their religious backgrounds. Their involvement in secular charities and causes demonstrates a broader commitment to social justice, human rights, and the welfare of society as a whole.

For instance, Safdar, who was passionate about his identity and the resting "good" face of Muslims, shared that his civic engaging went beyond Muslim issues. He shared,

> We did that a couple of times, and just recently, I went to a Black Lives Matter protest to protest the injustices against black people and minorities against the police brutality and the justice for George Floyd, who just passed away.

Kinza, who lives in the US, also shared that,

> I care about social justice in general . . . An example of a movement is Black Lives Matter, and something that I follow a lot, and police brutality. The meta moment, I guess, against sexual harassment and assault.

Salman explained his civic engagement was deeply tangled with climate change causes. He shared,

> I think, campaigning, I mean, I looked at this young girl from Finland, like Greta Thunberg, she is here and campaigning, and she is talking about the climate and everything like that, so I entered the campaign, and all these sorts of thing we really need to work on.

Nadimah also shared her participation in protests arranged to raise awareness regarding climate change in Australia. She noted,

> I have taken part in climate change rallies, I have taken part in anti-war protests, and that has just basically been because that is my way, interest, and that is what I am passionate about, and that is what I want to do.

Hasan admitted that he never went to any protests, but he did share posts and tried to raise awareness about climate change-related events. The young Australian noted,

> A lot of them hold climate change stuff. I haven't physically gone, but shared posts, liked posts, and things like that. But yeah, I have never actually gone to a proper protest.

The perception of Sharia among young Muslims varies when it comes to participating in civic activities. While Sharia itself does not prevent anyone from engaging in community service or civic participation, individuals interpret and prioritize its teachings differently based on their personal beliefs and values.

For some young Muslims, their faith acts as a motivating force that encourages them to take part in community services. They view it as a religious duty to help others, promote social justice, and contribute to the betterment of society. Their engagement in civic activities may be rooted in their understanding of Islamic teachings related to charity, compassion, and social responsibility.

On the other hand, there are those who are driven by "Muslim" causes due to identity politics. They may perceive a need to address issues specifically affecting the Muslim community, such as combating Islamophobia, promoting religious freedom, or advocating for Muslim rights. Their involvement in civic activities may be motivated by a desire to challenge stereotypes and discrimination (Yilmaz 2000, 2001), promote understanding, and create a more inclusive society for Muslims.

Furthermore, there are young Muslims who extend their ambitions beyond Muslim causes and engage in broader social issues. They recognize that their faith calls for justice and equality for all, and they feel compelled to address a range of pressing issues such as gender rights, ethnic violence, environmental concerns like climate change, poverty alleviation, and more. Their civic participation is driven by a desire to create positive change in various spheres, transcending religious boundaries and advocating for a more just and inclusive world.

7.6 Conclusion

While faith can be a significant factor for some, others may be driven by identity politics or a broader sense of social responsibility. The diverse range of causes and issues that young Muslims engage with demonstrates their active participation in shaping their communities and addressing pressing societal challenges, both within and beyond the scope of their religious identities.

The post-9/11 context undoubtedly had a significant impact on shaping the behaviour and attitudes of many young Muslims. However, as time has passed, it appears that the direct linkage between this context and their motivations has somewhat faded. Instead, a combination of factors such as faith, identity, democratic duty, and personal convictions now play a role in motivating their engagement in acts of citizenship.

When it came to voting, two distinct themes emerged among the participants. The first group, the Secular young Muslims, considers Islam or faith as a private matter that does not specifically encourage or discourage voting. Their voting decisions are primarily influenced by other factors such as personal preferences, party ideologies, or family traditions. Their detachment from faith-inspired behaviour and their fluidity in their attachment to faith on different issues could be attributed to their customized understanding and application of Sharia or a lack of clarity on its implications in certain fields.

One distinctive feature in terms of voting preferences that emerged was the voting behaviour of participants from Australia. Many of them mentioned voting either because it was compulsory or because they followed their family's voting patterns. Interestingly, only a few participants shared strong or detailed political opinions. In contrast, participants from the UK and the USA engaged in more in-depth discussions about voting and expressed their reasons for choosing particular candidates.

According to the interviewees, engagement within Muslim community organizations serves as a steppingstone towards further enriching their understanding of their role as active citizens. They offer a range of services, such as hosting newly migrated individuals or refugees, providing language courses, conducting capacity-building workshops, leadership programs, outreach activities, and interfaith dialogue initiatives, alongside their religious services.

The volunteer-driven nature of many of these activities provides participants with active ways to engage in civic activities. Furthermore, the sensitivity of these community organizations to social issues such as migration, unemployment, social security, and multiculturalism creates awareness of socio-political matters and encourages individuals to participate in voting or engage in local politics.

These findings are consistent with previous studies that have highlighted the multifaceted roles of mosques and the involvement of Muslim communities in Western countries. The activities and initiatives undertaken by these organizations not only contribute to the religious and cultural needs of the community but also foster civic engagement and political awareness among their members (Moutselos 2020; Fleischmann et al. 2016; McAndrew and Voas 2014; Bagby 2012; Jamal 2005).

The research highlights the concept of "acting citizenship" that goes beyond traditional forms of civic engagement, such as voting or volunteering. The themes that emerged from the study indicate that protesting and the idea of running for office were not unfamiliar to the participants. While some participants expressed their motivation for protesting as standing up for morally just causes, those inspired by Sharia teachings believed that Islam promotes the idea of social justice, making it a "duty" for Muslims to engage in protests.

It is not surprising that many participants felt compelled to protest against issues such as oppression in Palestine, Kashmir, and Burma that directly affect Muslims. However, what is notable is that many participants also felt connected to broader societal issues related to race, gender, and, at times, LGBTQ rights. For some, engaging in protests was seen as exercising their democratic liberties, while others believed their faith motivated them to take a stand on these matters.

This highlights the multifaceted nature of civic participation among young Muslims, where their motivations can stem from both democratic principles and religious beliefs. The participants' sense of duty to address social justice issues reflects their understanding of Islam's teachings and their desire to advocate for justice and equality. By participating in protests, they actively express their concerns and work towards creating positive change in society, aligning their actions with their faith-inspired values.

This research contributes to the understanding that civic engagement among young Muslims is not limited to specific issues but encompasses a broad range of causes that they perceive as morally significant, whether directly related to their religious identity or not. It demonstrates the intersectionality of their engagement, where they connect with various social justice issues and leverage their democratic liberties to voice their concerns and work towards a more inclusive and just society.

The study findings indicate that young Muslims did not feel that Islam prohibited them from running for office or participating in democratic politics. While some participants expressed uncertainty about this issue, it was often attributed to the perceived corrupt nature of politics, which they felt conflicted with the teachings of Islam. On the other hand, many participants expressed satisfaction and support for the representation of Muslims in local, state, and national governments, particularly in the UK, where there is a higher presence of people of colour and faith in politics. However, regional differences played a role, with participants from Australia and, to some extent, the US feeling that more representation was needed.

Overall, the study highlights that acting on various citizenship ideas and engaging in civic participation is common among the sampled young Muslims. Those who were motivated by Sharia-driven thinking to perform these acts did not express displeasure with the democratic system but rather saw their faith as a complimentary companion that coexisted with it. Simultaneously, there is a clear presence of young Muslims who feel that their spiritual belief systems are entirely disengaged from their civic acts. This diversity of perspectives and motivations within the Muslim community underscores the complexity and individuality of their experiences and attitudes towards civic participation.

References

Bagby, I. 2009. The American Mosque in Transition: Assimilation, Acculturation, and Isolation. *Journal of Ethnic and Migration Studies, 35*(3), 473–490. CrossRef-Google Scholar

Bagby, I. 2012. The American Mosque 2011. *Council on American-Islamic Relations: US Mosque Study 2011*, 1–29. www.icna.org/wp-content/uploads/2012/02/The-American-Mosque-2011-web.pdf.Google Scholar

Barton, G., Weller, P., & Yilmaz, I. 2013. *The Muslim World and Politics in Transition: Creative Contributions of the Gülen Movement*. Bloomsbury Publishers.

Fleischmann, F., Martinovic, B., & Böhm, M. 2016. Mobilising Mosques? The Role of Service Attendance for Political Participation of Turkish and Moroccan Minorities in the Netherlands. *Ethnic and Racial Studies, 39*(5), 746–763. https://doi.org/10.1080/01419870.2015.1081962

Isin, E. F., & Nielsen, G. M. (Eds.). 2008. *Acts of Citizenship*. Bloomsbury Publishing.

Jamal, A. 2005. The Political Participation and Engagement of Muslim Americans: Mosque Involvement and Group Consciousness. *American Politics Research, 33*(4), 521–544. https://doi.org/10.1177/1532673X04271385

McAndrew, S., & Voas, D. 2014. Immigrant Generation, Religiosity and Civic Engagement in Britain. *Ethnic and Racial Studies, 37*(1), 99–119. https://doi.org/10.1080/01419870.2013.808755

Moutselos, M. 2020. Praying on Friday, Voting on Sunday? Mosque Attendance and Voter Turnout in Three West European Democracies. *Journal of Ethnic and Migration Studies, 46*(11), 2275–2292. https://doi.org/10.1080/1369183X.2019.1662283

Yilmaz, I. 2000. Muslim Law in Britain, Reflections in the Socio-Legal Sphere and Differential Legal Treatment. *Journal of Muslim Minority Affairs, 20*(2), 353–360. https://doi.org/10.1080/713680357

Yilmaz, I. 2001. Law as Chameleon: The Question of Incorporation of Muslim Personal Law into the English Law. *Journal of Muslim Minority Affairs, 21*(2), 297–308.

Yilmaz, I. 2012. Towards a Muslim Secularism? An Islamic "Twin Tolerations" Understanding of Religion in the Public Sphere. *Turkish Journal of Politics, 3*(2), 41–52.

Yilmaz, I. 2023a. *Islam in the Anglosphere: Perspectives of Young Muslims in Australia, the UK and the USA*. Palgrave Macmillan.

Yilmaz, I. 2023b. Muslim Secularism by Conduct: Attitudes of Young Australian Muslims to Legal Pluralism and Sharia. *Journal of Intercultural Studies, 44*(2), 274–288. https://doi.org/10.1080/07256868.2022.2104826

Weller, P., & Yilmaz, I. 2012. *European Muslims, Civility and Public Life: Perspectives On and From the Gülen Movement*. Continuum Publishers.

8 Understanding Sharia in Western Contexts

Insights from Young Muslims

This book investigates Sharia's relevance to young Muslims living in Western countries. It aims to explore how Sharia-driven laws and practices manifest in the daily lives of Muslims, highlighting the diversity of opinions within the Muslim community. Unlike relying solely on mass media or seeking explanations from religious scholars, the book examines the applied side of Sharia through in-depth interviews with young Muslims from Australia, the United States, and the United Kingdom. It is important to acknowledge that the study primarily focusses on participants from these three English-speaking countries and major metropolitan areas. This limits the representation of non-English speaking Western countries and variations in experiences based on rural-urban differences. Further research is needed to capture the perspectives of individuals from a wider range of Western countries and diverse socio-cultural contexts to gain a more comprehensive understanding of the subject matter.

By conducting interviews with participants from these Western countries and diverse backgrounds, the book seeks to provide a comprehensive understanding of the varied perspectives and experiences related to Sharia. It aims to shed light on how Muslims navigate and interpret Sharia in their day-to-day lives, moving beyond stereotypes and generalizations. Through first-hand accounts and personal narratives, the book offers insights into the multifaceted nature of Sharia and its impact on the lives of young Muslims.

The book's first finding highlights the existence of pluralism within the debate surrounding legal pluralism among the participants. The categorization of Legal Pluralist A and B and Muslim Secular A and B demonstrates the diversity of thoughts and perspectives on the subject. Additionally, the study reveals that while young Muslims are willing to share their opinions about Sharia, many of them also express uncertainty about the concept. They often make educated guesses about its implications, mirroring the broader theological debate surrounding Sharia. This lack of a clear definition of Sharia is evident among young Muslims as well.

The study also highlights the highly stigmatized nature of discussing Sharia in the post-9/11 world as participants navigate the societal perceptions and stereotypes associated with the topic. It further explores the relationship between faith and identity, with some participants considering faith as central

DOI: 10.4324/9781003482604-8

to their identity while others attribute its centrality to societal factors. Notably, participants from the UK and the US exhibited more confidence in discussing Sharia compared to those from Australia, although the reasons for this disparity are not explicitly mentioned.

The study provides insights into the dynamics of seeking guidance from imams among young Muslims, both through traditional consultations and online. It goes beyond examining the mere act of consultation and delves deeper into the factors influencing the choice of imams and the nature of the exchange. One important finding is that ethnicity and race do not significantly impact the selection of an imam. Instead, considerations such as the imam's perspective on modern issues, their understanding of Western contexts, and even their sectarian orientation play a role. This indicates that young Muslims actively seek out imams who align with their progressive values and can relate to their experiences rather than being influenced solely by biases or dogmatic beliefs. A noteworthy observation from the study is the barriers faced by women when it comes to freely consulting an imam. This highlights the need for further research to explore the unique dynamics and challenges experienced by women and sectarian minorities in seeking guidance from imams. Understanding these differences can contribute to a more comprehensive understanding of the role of imams in the lives of young Muslims.

The study also highlights the significant role of the internet in information-seeking among young Muslims, particularly in relation to religious guidance. While the internet, often humorously referred to as "Sheikh Google," is a commonly used platform to seek information, the participants acknowledge its limitations and the need for authentication. This indicates that young Muslims recognize the importance of verifying information obtained through online searches and have strategies to ensure the reliability of the sources they consult.

The study also brings attention to the emergence of e-imams, who are transnational, young, and Western-educated religious figures. These e-imams have gained popularity among young Muslims due to their relatability and approachability. They have become viral hits and serve as a source of Sharia for many. This finding raises interesting questions about the appeal and influence of these e-imams, which warrant further exploration.

Future studies could study the process young Muslims use to authenticate information obtained online and the factors influencing their trust in specific sources on online platforms. Additionally, investigating the characteristics and strategies employed by e-imams that make them influential and resonate with young Muslims would provide valuable insights into the evolving landscape of religious guidance in the digital age.

The study reveals that in addition to formal sources such as imams and online platforms, young Muslims also rely on informal sources within their social networks for religious guidance. Family members, university scholars, and knowledgeable friends play a significant role in answering religious questions and providing insights into Sharia-related matters. This finding highlights the existence of a micro-dynamic sphere of religious discourse and consultation within the broader debates surrounding legal pluralism.

The reliance on these informal sources indicates the importance of interpersonal relationships and personal connections in shaping the understanding and practice of Sharia among young Muslims. It suggests that individuals seek guidance from individuals they trust and have close relationships with, which may provide a more personalized and contextualized understanding of Sharia.

This aspect of the study emphasizes the need to consider the diverse range of sources that young Muslims engage with in their quest for religious knowledge. It adds another layer to the understanding of the complexities and dynamics involved in the formation and transmission of Sharia-driven practices within the Muslim community.

Further research could analyze the role of informal sources, exploring the nature of these interpersonal relationships, the dynamics of knowledge-sharing within social networks, and the influence they have on individual interpretations and practices of Sharia. Such investigations would contribute to a more comprehensive understanding of the multifaceted nature of legal pluralism and the diverse pathways through which Sharia-related knowledge is acquired and disseminated among young Muslims.

The study also looks into the relationship between Sharia-driven thinking and acts of citizenship among Muslims in the West. It uncovers a divide among the participants, with legal pluralists perceiving Islam as compatible with and even encouraging civic participation such as voting and protesting. However, some individuals within this group express uncertainty about the purity or morality of politics and its compatibility with Islam. This connection between Sharia-driven thinking and civic engagement presents an intriguing avenue for future studies to explore further. On the other hand, there is a segment of Muslims who identify as secular and do not feel motivated by their faith to participate in acts of citizenship actively. This highlights the diversity within the Muslim community in terms of their engagement with civic activities.

Young Muslims frequently seek guidance and clarification from imams on various political issues. Additionally, many participants feel a strong connection to transnational Muslim causes such as Kashmir and Palestine. There is also a small but notable portion of individuals interested in advocating for racial justice and gender equity, suggesting a convergence of transnational issues with local community concerns. These findings open up discussions on how young Muslims in the West align themselves with transnational issues and forge alliances within their local communities. It provides valuable insights into the complexities of Muslim civic engagement and the various factors, including Sharia-driven thinking and transnational solidarity, that shape their activism and participation in broader social and political movements.

In summary, this book presented in-depth interviews with young Muslims living as a minority in liberal democracies to highlight their experiences and perspectives. It explored the diversity of views regarding Sharia and its influence on their lives. The presence of legal pluralism does not hinder the ability of young Muslims to participate actively in their multicultural societies. In fact, it often helps them in practicing their religious rituals and can also motivate them to engage as active citizens. The study also reveals that young Muslims demonstrate a sense of agency and practicality by being cautious in sourcing religious information. Overall, the book provided insights into the dynamic lives of young Muslims and their navigation of religious and civic identities within Western contexts.

These Muslims often feel pressured to conform to certain expectations and behaviours imposed on them due to these biases. Despite advocating for the compatibility of Islamic laws and morals with existing legal systems, it is important to note that legal pluralists do not generally promote overthrowing liberal democracies. Instead, they see Islamic principles as complementary to the values and laws already in place. Some even argue that incorporating Islamic laws would benefit humanity and make their lives easier.

However, one of the challenges highlighted in the study is the lack of understanding and clarity surrounding the concept of Sharia among legal pluralists. This ambiguity makes it difficult for them to determine the actual implications of legalizing Sharia in their respective countries. While the intentions of legal pluralists may be positive, their limited understanding of Sharia and vague ideas about its implementation raise concerns about the potential consequences of such actions.

Appendix

Table 1.0 Ethnicity of Australian, British, and American Muslims and Sample Size

Australian Sample		
Ethnicity	***Self-Identified Ethnicity***	***No.***
	Iraqi	8
	Pakistani	7
	Turkish	7
	Lebanese	6
	Indian	5
	Afghan	5
	Indonesian	4
	Bosnian	3
	Palestinian	2
	Iranian	2
	Bangladeshi	2
	Malay-Singaporean	1
	Indian-Singaporean	1
	Indian-South-African	1
	Pakistani-Fijian	1
	Palestinian-Lebanese	1
	Arab-Afghan	1
	Uighur	1
	Kurdish	1
	Sri Lankan	1
	Kenyan	1
	Turkish-Macedonian	1
	Albanian	1
	Anglo-Australian	1
American Sample		
Ethnicity	***Self-Identified Ethnicity***	***No.***
	Albanian	4
	Albanian + White	1
	Turkish	4
	Turkish + Azeri	1
	Tajik/Kyrgyz	1
	Bulgarian	1
	African	2

(*Continued*)

Table 1.0 (Continued)

American Sample		
	African American	1
	American	2
	Black + Puerto Rican	1
	American + Caucasian/White	1
	Arab	1
	Moroccan	1
	Iraqi-Kurdish	1
	Arab + American + Latin American	1
	South Asian	2
	Bengali	1
	Pakistani	1
	Pakistani + Indian	1
	South Asian Pakistani	1
	Pakistani-American	1
British Sample		
Ethnicity	***Self-Identified Ethnicity***	***No.***
	British-Pakistani	13
	British-Bangladeshi	5
	Kurdish-Irish	1
	British-Turkish	1
	White British Asian	1
	British-Libyan	1
	Mauritian	1
	Mixed Race	1
	Turkish-Syrian	1
	Turkish-Yemeni	1
	Not identified	2

Index

Made in the USA
Las Vegas, NV
19 September 2026

703f7177-4691-40d8-8f01-fbbf102d2dc8R01